James J. Moriarty

Stumbling-Blocks Made Stepping-Stones

On the Road to the Catholic faith

James J. Moriarty

Stumbling-Blocks Made Stepping-Stones
On the Road to the Catholic faith

ISBN/EAN: 9783337375508

Printed in Europe, USA, Canada, Australia, Japan

Cover: Foto ©Lupo / pixelio.de

More available books at **www.hansebooks.com**

STUMBLING-BLOCKS

MADE

STEPPING-STONES

ON THE ROAD TO THE

CATHOLIC FAITH.

BY THE

REV. JAMES J. MORIARTY, A.M.,

Pastor of St. Patrick's Church, Chatham Village, New York.

"DIVERSO STYLO, NON DIVERSA FIDE."

"Sanctify the Lord Christ in your hearts, being always ready to satisfy every one that asketh you a reason of that hope which is in you."
1 EPIST. ST. PETER iii. 15.

NEW YORK
THE CATHOLIC PUBLICATION SOCIETY CO.,
9 BARCLAY STREET.
—
1880.

TO

MY PROTESTANT FRIENDS AND FELLOW-CITIZENS,

WHOSE

CANDOR, LOVE OF TRUTH, AND OPENNESS TO CONVICTION

HAVE ALWAYS WON MY ADMIRATION,

THIS HUMBLE WORK

IS SINCERELY DEDICATED,

WITH THE HOPE

THAT IT MAY SERVE TO DISPEL THE MISTS OF PREJUDICE

AND LEAD THE WAY

TO A

GREATER ILLUMINATION FROM THE FATHER OF LIGHT,

"THE GIVER OF EVERY GOOD AND PERFECT GIFT."

CONTENTS.

	PAGE.
Preface, ...	. 7
The Sacrifice of the Mass and its Ceremonies,	. 13
The Confessional, ...	. 58
The Invocation of Saints, ...	. 101
Devotion to the Blessed Virgin Mary, . .	. 139
Purgatory, ...	. 185
Infallibility, ...	. 235

PREFACE.

A FEW words with my kind readers may not, I hope, be deemed out of place. Instructed by an experience of fourteen years in a widely-extended mission—within the limits of which the members of the Catholic religion are in a marked minority—the writer of this little work has found, during his frequent and almost daily intercourse with those not of the household of faith, that most of the objections against the Church are grounded on mistaken notions concerning those salient points of her teaching which he here endeavors to elucidate.

To many persons the "Mass" seems an unmeaning sort of pantomime, the "Confessional" a huge imposition, the "Intercession of Saints" an unwarranted innovation, "Devotion to the Blessed Virgin" despicable idolatry, "Purgatory" an impious fraud, and "Infallibility" absolute despotism. Therefore it is that he has selected these in preference to other doctrines, as they have been more assailed and more misunderstood.

The writer puts no faith in mere controversy. He believes in the necessity of clear, simple, earnest explanations of Catholic dogmas, with the absence of every expression that could possibly wound or offend. Controversies are seldom or never productive of good results. They only serve to stir up bad feeling, to excite still more bitterly the prejudices of both sides, and to render the disputants still more tenacious of their own ground.

Explanation enlightens and does not disturb, removes difficulties and does not wound, softens asperities and leaves no trace of bitterness behind.

Much as we may, and do, differ on points of faith, and fundamental ones too, it is no reason that we should bear ill-feeling to one another. We should hate error, heresy, and every compromise of truth with falsehood, but we should by no means hate those in error or in heresy, but embrace them all in the charity of Christ, praying for their conversion and removing all obstacles from their path.

A great and glorious destiny not only in the material, but also in the spiritual, order is in store for this nation. This is the great country of the future, not only for liberty but also for religion. Here the great battle between faith and infidelity is to be waged.

The principles of the Catholic religion are in full harmony with those enunciated in the Declaration of Independence. There is no danger of incompatibility; and if our priests and people be but fully alive to a sense of their great responsibilities, long before the next centennial of our national existence 'shall dawn this grand Republic will be the stronghold of the Church of God.

Animated with these views, and trusting in the goodness of that God who wishes all men to be saved and to arrive at the knowledge of truth, I calmly let loose this little venturesome craft on the dangerous ocean of the literary world, hoping that it may serve as a temporary help and support for some poor mariner tossed about on the sea of doubt and carried away by every wind of doctrine, until he may be able to give true signals and hail the precious life-boat of Peter and be wafted in safety to the everlasting shore.

J. J. M.

CHATHAM VILLAGE, N. Y.,
FEAST OF ST. MARTIN OF TOURS,
November 11, 1879.

I.

THE SACRIFICE OF THE MASS, AND ITS CEREMONIES.

THE Mass is the key to the entire Catholic worship—the sun or centre of the whole Catholic system. Understand it fully and clearly, and everything connected with the ceremonial of the Church becomes perfectly plain and full of divine meaning.

Be in ignorance with regard to its proper explanation, and everything in Catholic worship becomes unintelligible—a mere pantomime, a senseless jargon.

Comprehend it, as the Church understands it and wishes it to be understood, and it is the grandest action that can be possibly performed in the universe. God himself, with all the unlimited capabilities of His omnipotence, could not bestow on man the power to perform a nobler, holier, or more important function.

There is not a single motion, a minute ceremony, an apparently insignificant vestment, not the slightest change of posture, not a movement nor a prayer, that has not its deep mystic meaning, that carries not with it its useful lesson, its cheering thought, its consoling promise, or its earnest exhortation.

How sublime, and even divine, is the Mass!

No matter how retired the locality, how miserably poor the surroundings, or how humble the roof under which it is celebrated — *there* is an action performed which rivets the attention and claims the worship of even the highest of those blessed spirits who watch over this material world of ours.

Behold the priest vested for the Holy Sacrifice—the priest another Christ (*Sacerdos, alter Christus*), as he has been well termed. Hear him giving forth the moving forty-second psalm, "Judica"; see him bowed down in the profound humiliation of the "Confiteor"; then, ascending the Holy of Holies, thrice begging pardon of each of the three Divine Persons of the adorable Trinity at the "Kyrie," intoning with joyous strain the glorious anthem of the angelic "Gloria," announcing the sublime doctrines of the "Gospel," proclaiming aloud the potent "Credo," offering up the precious elements at the "Offertory," raising his heart and those of his hearers at the "Sursum corda" of the Preface, and the exultant "Sanctus"; witness the worshipful adoration at the "Consecration," the silent absorption of the "Memento," the prayer of the Incarnate God, the divine "Pater Noster," the humble centurion's "Domine, non sum dignus," the soul-absorbing consuming of the Sacred Species at the Communion, and the last blessing, in the name of the omnipotent God, of the assembled prayerful multitude!

What possibly could be grander or more soul-inspiring than this tremendous mystery—*tremendum mysterium*, as it is called by the Council of Trent?

Before entering on an explanation of what the Mass is, on what foundations it rests, the meaning of its sacred ceremonies, and the vestments used in its celebration, a few words on the nature and history of

SACRIFICES

in general will not, I trust, be out of place.

A sacrifice is an offering, by a legitimate minister, of something which falls under the senses and which undergoes destruction or change, in acknowledgment of the supreme dominion of God over all creatures.

From the very beginning of the world sacrifices were offered to the Almighty, and can certainly be traced back to the immediate sons of Adam, Abel and Cain —the former offering to God the firstlings of his flock, and the latter the firstfruits of the earth. Noe offered his sacrifice after coming out of the ark; Abraham, his beloved son Isaac, the type of Christ; Melchisedech, bread and wine

—the figure of the Eucharistic Sacrifice, or the Mass. Melchisedech, "the king of justice and of peace," was a true type of Christ. He was called "Priest of the Most High," and to him Abraham paid tithes of all the spoils gained by his victory over the kings. Sacred Scripture gives no genealogy of Melchisedech, who rejoiced in the priestly office, inherited from no one and not succeeded to by others.

In all times and countries, even when and where the worship of the true God was abandoned, sacrifices were offered by all tribes and peoples to their divinities. Being no doubt a part of the primitive revelation made to mankind, it seems to have been a natural instinct of the human heart to offer up some sacrifice—such as the blood of animals or the firstfruits of the earth—in acknowledgment of the supreme dominion of God over life and death.

Amongst the Greeks, the Romans, the Persians, and even amongst the most barbarous and uncivilized people in our own times, this custom prevailed and still prevails. By all it was looked upon as an essential act of worship, as a necessary act consequent upon man's dependence on God, and also as the most efficacious means of appeasing an angry Deity.

Such has been the constant and invariable belief even of those left to their own natural light and not gifted with that superior light of divine faith illumining from on high.

All the sacrifices under the Law of Moses were more or less symbolical of the great Sacrifice of the New Law. All were commanded by God Himself, who prescribed the various ceremonies to be performed during the holy functions.

THE SACRIFICE OF THE NEW LAW,

which was once offered up in a bloody manner on Calvary's Mount by Jesus Christ Himself, who was both High-Priest and Victim, is ever since continued and renewed, though offered up in an unbloody manner, on all our altars, and shall so continue unto the end of time.

The Sacrifice of the Mass and the Sacrifice on Calvary are not two different sacrifices, therefore, but one and the same, having the same High-Priest and the same adorable Victim. In the Sacrifice of Calvary Our Blessed Saviour suffered a real death; in that of the

Mass, a *mystical* death, represented by the separate consecration of the sacred species, the bread and the wine. This sacrifice has, consequently, the same effect as that of Calvary, and the figurative death of our Lord, together with the participation of His Sacred Flesh and Blood, is as wonderfully productive of grace and power as the real, true death once consummated on the ignominious gibbet of the Cross. His sacrifice was not to be transitory or of short duration, but intended to continue during all time, in every age and country, as may be clearly seen from the prophecies of the Old Testament and His own unmistakable declarations in the New Testament.

The Almighty, expressing Himself displeased with the sacrifices of the Jews, foretold, through

THE PROPHET MALACHIAS,

the new oblation which would be offered among the Gentiles, and which would render glory to His Name. He announces this new and great Sacrifice—one entirely worthy of Him—which would not be offered in one particular place, but amongst all nations "from the rising to the setting of the sun." "I have no pleasure in you, saith the Lord of Hosts, and I will not receive a gift of your hand. For from the rising of the sun even to the going down, My Name is great among the Gentiles; and in every place there is sacrifice, and there is offered to My Name a clean oblation: for My Name is great among the Gentiles, saith the Lord of Hosts" (Malachias i. 10, 11).

The same oblation was prefigured in the old law, as we learn from the Book of Genesis, xiv. 18: "Melchisedech, the king of Salem, bringing forth bread and wine, for he was the priest of the Most High God."

The Psalmist testifies to the same (Psalm cix. 4): "The Lord hath sworn, and He will not repent: Thou art a priest for ever according to the order of Melchisedech."

The great Apostle St. Paul, in his Epistle to the Hebrews, thus gives his testimony: "It is impossible that with the blood of oxen and goats sins should be taken away. Therefore, coming into the world he saith: Sacrifice and oblation thou wouldst not; but a body thou hast fitted to me; holocausts for sin did not please thee. Then said I: Behold,

I come; in the head of the book it is written of me, that I should do Thy will, O God. . . . He taketh away the first, that he may establish that which followeth" (x. 4-9).

Then we have the Evangelist's testimony, than which nothing can be more clear: "And taking bread He gave thanks, and brake: and gave to them, saying: This is My Body which is given for you. Do this for a commemoration of Me. In like manner the chalice also, after He had supped, saying: This is the chalice of the new testament in My Blood, which shall be shed for you" (St. Luke xxii. 19-22).

It is evident from this last text that our Blessed Saviour commanded the apostles, and in them their successors in office, to continue to offer up this saving

Victim until the end of time. His sacrifice was to be offered but once in that terribly painful and bloody manner, as it was on Calvary's mount for the sins of all mankind; but it is His intention that the same great sacrifice should be continued as long as His Church should last—that is, unto the consummation of ages—and be offered up, in an unbloody manner, in order that the merits of redemption should be applied to our souls. In other words, the grand *offering* for the sins of the human race was made in the sacrifice of Calvary, but the *application* of the same infinite merits is effected through the Sacrifice of the Mass.

St. Paul says (Heb. xiii. 10): "We have an altar, whereof they have no power to eat who serve the tabernacle."

What use would there be for an *altar* without a *priest?* And what utility to be derived from both priest and altar, if there were no sacrifice to be offered?

The same great apostolic teacher warns the Christians to beware of participating in the sacrifice offered to idols, as they would then be unworthy of participating in the Christian sacrifice.

"I would not that you should be made partakers with devils. You cannot drink the chalice of the Lord, and the chalice of devils: you cannot be partakers of the table of the Lord, and of the table of devils" (1 Corinthians x. 20, 21). "The chalice of benediction, which we bless, is it not the communion of the blood of Christ? And the bread, which we break, is it not the partaking of the body of the Lord?" (Ibid. 16). Also in the eleventh chapter of the same beautiful epistle: "For I have received of the Lord that which also I delivered unto you, that the Lord Jesus, the night in which He was betrayed, took bread, and giving thanks, broke and said: Take ye and eat: this is My Body which shall be delivered for you; do this for the commemoration of Me. In like manner also the chalice, after He had supped, saying: This chalice is the new testament in My blood; this do ye, as often as ye shall drink, for the commemoration of Me. For as often as ye shall eat this bread, and drink the chalice, ye shall show the death of the Lord, until He come. Therefore, whosoever shall eat this bread, or drink the chalice of the Lord unworthily, shall be guilty of the body and blood of the Lord. But let a man prove himself: and so let him eat of that bread and drink of the chalice. For he that eateth and drinketh unworthily, eateth and drinketh judgment to himself, not discerning the Body of the Lord." (All these texts are substantially the same in the Protestant version of the Scriptures.)

The Sacrifice of the Mass derives all its merit, power, and efficacy from the Sacrifice of the Cross, the latter being the source of grace, and the former the channel through which it comes to us. On the Cross the infinite merits of Jesus Christ became our property, but in the Mass this inexhaustible wealth is distributed throughout the world. On the Cross He died for all men in general; in the Mass, special application is made to individual souls.

The Mass, being a supreme act of worship, can only be offered to

GOD ALONE.

"Deus, cui offertur; Deus, qui offertur; Deus, a quo offertur." As St. Augustine says: "God, to whom it is offered; God, who is offered; God, by whom it is offered."

It cannot be offered to any created being, not to the highest saint or the brightest angel; no, not even to the Blessed Virgin. Mass may be, and often is, offered to the Almighty in honor of the Blessed Virgin, the angels, or the saints, in order to thank Him for the great graces and glory bestowed upon them and to beg their intercession, that we may follow in their footsteps and cultivate those virtues which they possessed in so high a degree; but the Mass is never offered *to* any saint, howsoever elevated, for this would be an act of idolatry—the giving to a creature the worship due only to the Creator.

"Idolatry," says Dr. Jeremy Taylor, the great divine of the Church of England (in his book entitled *Liberty of Prophesying*, section 20, m. 26), "is a forsaking the true God and giving divine worship to a creature, or to an idol—that is, to an imaginary god. Now, it is evident that the object of their [the Catholics'] devotion in the Blessed Sacrament is the only true and Eternal God, hypostatically joined with His holy humanity, which humanity they believe actually present under the veil of the sacramental signs. And if they thought Him not present, they are so far from worshipping the bread in this case, they themselves profess it idolatry to do so. Which is a demonstration that their soul has nothing in it which is idolatrical; the will has nothing in it but what is a great enemy to idolatry; and nothing burns in hell but proper will."

The Mass, then, is an offering made to the Almighty of the Body and Blood of Jesus Christ, or an action in which bread is consecrated into the Body and wine into the Blood of Christ by the sacred ministry of the priest, using the very words of our Saviour, and gifted with His authority, in commemoration of the sacrifice of Calvary, "to show the death of the Lord until He come."

From all that has been said the conclusion is evident that the value of the Mass is infinite. St. Alphonsus Liguori declares that "all the honor which angels by their adoration, men by their good works, austerities, and even martyrdom, have ever rendered or ever shall render to God, never could and never will give him so much glory as one single Mass; for while the honor of all creatures is only finite, that which accrues to God from the Holy Sacrifice of the altar is infinite, insomuch as the Victim which is offered is of infinite value. The Mass, therefore, offers to God the greatest honor that can be given Him; subdues most triumphantly the powers of hell; affords the greatest relief to the souls in purgatory; appeases most efficaciously the wrath of God against sinners, and brings down the greatest blessings on mankind."

" This is truly the corn of the elect, and the wine springing forth virgins " (Zach. ix. 17).

St. Bonaventure calls the Mass " the compendium of all God's benefits " — *compendium quoddam beneficiorum suorum.* St. John Chrysostom says that the Mass has as much value as the death of Christ on the cross: *Tantum valet celebratio Missæ quantum valet mors Christi in cruce.*

"Oh! how greatly to be revered the dignity of priests," says the great St. Augustine in his commentary on the twenty-seventh psalm, "in whose hands, as in the womb of the Virgin, the Son of God takes unto Himself flesh " —*O veneranda sacerdotum dignitas, in quorum manibus velut in utero Virginis Filius Dei incarnatur*

CEREMONIES OF THE MASS.

In all public worship ceremonies have always been considered necessary for the proper performance of sacred functions, and for the maintenance of greater decency and propriety. Some form of ceremonial law has ever been in use from patriarchal times, and still more so under the law of Moses; the various vestments and ceremonies having been ordained by God Himself. Nor did our Blessed Saviour disdain the use of ceremonies, as we perceive from those He employed when He cured the man born blind (John xv. 6) and the deaf and dumb (Mark vii. 33). They are calculated, first, to preserve uniformity, so desirable in divine worship; secondly, to demonstrate, by exterior action, the interior dispositions of the soul, owing, as we do, the worship of both body and soul to the Almighty; moreover, in the third place, these outward ceremonies bring to mind, and more deeply impress, the truth of Christian mysteries, the dispositions required for the proper reception of the sacraments, and the corresponding obligations which they impose.

Many of the ceremonies were instituted by the Apostles and their immediate successors, "for the edification of the body of Christ" (Eph. iv). "Let all things be done decently and according to order," says St. Paul (1 Cor. xiv. 40). "The rest I will set in order when I come" (1 Cor. xi. 34). These words show that the apostle no doubt established regulations for the proper maintenance of divine worship.

Now let us come to an explanation of the vestments of the priest and the ceremonies of the Mass.

THE PRIEST

is dressed in vestments every one of which is symbolical, having reference chiefly to the Passion of Christ, whose representative he is, more especially during the Holy Sacrifice.

The first article which he puts on is a small, white, oblong linen cloth, which he first places on the back of his head and allows to fall on his shoulders close to the neck. This is the *amict*, and represents the rags with which the Jews muffled our Saviour's face. The *alb* (the long white garment extending to the feet and covering the cassock or soutane, the priest's ordinary ecclesiastical dress) is emblematic of the white garment put in derision on our Lord by Herod. The cincture, or girdle, signifies the cords and bands by which He was bound. The *maniple* (from the Latin word *manus*, the hand) is worn on the left arm in memory of the cords with which His hands were tied to the pillar during the scourging. The *stole*, worn round the neck with the extremities crossed over the priest's breast, signifies the heavy yoke of the cross to which He submitted for our sakes. The *chasuble*, the full outer vestment, the purple garment with which our Saviour was clothed in mockery in the court of Pontius Pilate. On the *chasuble* is always a large embroidered cross, to remind both priest and people that the efficacy of the Sacrifice of the altar is derived from that of the Cross on Calvary. The *berretta*, or square black cap of the priest, is symbolical of the crown of thorns.

The *altar* represents Mount Calvary; the *chalice*, the sepulchre; the altar linens, the winding-sheets; the *paten* or silver plate, the stone rolled against the entrance of the sepulchre; and the candles, the light of faith, "without which it is impossible to please God."

The vestments have also a mystic meaning in reference to the priest himself. The *amict* denotes divine hope, "the helmet of salvation"; the *alb*, innocence of life; the *cincture*, holy purity; the *maniple*, patience in suffering; the *stole*, the yoke of Christ—"My yoke is sweet indeed and my burden light"; and the *chasuble*, covering all the rest, the great mantle of charity.

The vestments are of different colors. *White*, emblematic of purity, is used on the joyous feasts of our Lord, the Blessed Virgin, the confessors and virgins. *Red*, significative of fortitude, on the feasts of the Holy Cross, the instruments of the Passion, during the octave of Pentecost, and on the feasts of the martyrs. *Purple* is used in Lent and other penitential seasons. *Green* (expressive of hope) is used on ordinary Sundays from octave of Epiphany to Septuagesima and from octave of Pentecost to Advent, when there is no special feast. *Black* is used in Masses for the dead and on Good Friday.

THE DIFFERENT PARTS OF THE MASS.

The Mass, as well as every office of religion, begins with the sign of the cross: *In nomine Patris et Filii et Spiritus Sancti. Amen.*—"In the name of the Father, and of the Son, and of the Holy Ghost." Amen. The Unity and Trinity of God, the Incarnation, Passion, and Death of our Saviour are all expressed by this one saving sign. No wonder, then, that it has been in such constant use from the time of Christ and His Apostles.

Tertullian, who wrote in the second century of our era, thus speaks of it: "At every moving from place to place, at every coming in and going out; in dressing, at the baths, at table; on lighting candles, going to rest, sitting down; in whatever action we are engaged, we sign ourselves on the forehead with the cross" (*De Corona Mil.*)

The priest then recites the forty-second psalm, "Judica" (the forty-third in the Protestant version), expressing the joy and desires of a soul approaching the altar of God. Bowing down, he says the "Confiteor," or general confession, in humble acknowledgment of his sinfulness before God, and the clerk or acolyte does the same on behalf of the people—showing the necessity of true repentance in order to derive the fruits of the Great Sacrifice.

Ascending the altar steps, he begs of God to take away our iniquities, that we may be fit to enter His sanctuary.

He then begins the Mass of the day at the "Introit" (an anthem from some part of the Scriptures, with verse of psalm and Gloria Patri), after which he returns to the middle of the altar, where he says " Kyrie eleison " (the Greek for " Lord, have mercy ") thrice to God the Father, " Christe eleison " thrice to God the Son, and " Kyrie eleison " thrice to God the Holy Ghost.

He then (except in penitential times, votive Masses, and Masses for the dead) intones the " Gloria in excelsis "—" Glory be to God on high." This hymn of praise being concluded, he turns to the people and says: " Dominus vobiscum " —" The Lord be with you." This salutation is made seven times during the Mass, and is the same as was addressed to Gedeon by the angel (Judges vi. 12), to the reapers by Boaz (Ruth ii. 4), and to Asa by Azarias (2 Paral. xv. 2).

After one or more prayers at the left-hand side of the altar, he then reads the " Epistle," which is selected from some one of the various epistles of the New or from some book of the Old Testament, which being concluded, the acolyte says: "Deo gratias," or "Thanks to God," for these salutary instructions.

The missal or mass-book is then changed to the gospel side of the altar, denoting the change from the Old to the New Dispensation, and the people always stand while the Gospel is being read, to show their firm belief in the word of God and their readiness to obey it.

Before the reading of the Gospel both priest and people make the sign of the cross on their foreheads to testify their open profession of the faith, on their lips to show that they are willing to give testimony to the same by their words, and on their breasts that they wish to cultivate it with their heart's best affections. At the conclusion of the Gospel the acolyte says, or the choir chants, "Laus tibi, Christe," "Praise to Thee, O Christ," for vouchsafing to teach us such heavenly doctrines.

Then (on Sundays and special feasts) the "Creed" is intoned, that creed which has been recited in the Church since the time of the Councils of Nice and Constantinople, and when the celebrant says the words "et incarnatus est," he and all present bend the knee in honor of the Incarnation of the Divine Word.

At the "Offertory" of the bread and wine the priest begs of the Almighty to accept the sacrifice, which he is about to offer, for the remission of his own sins and those of the people, and for the refreshment of all those souls who departed this life in the peace and friendship of God. He blesses the bread and wine, and beseeches the Holy Spirit to sanctify them unto His Holy Name.

Proceeding to the epistle side, he washes the tips of those fingers which are to hold the Sacred Host, at the same time reciting the "Lavabo" (the twenty-fifth psalm), denoting the purity of body and soul with which we should assist at so holy an action.

Returning to the middle of the altar, he there bows down, begging of the ever-blessed Trinity to receive this offering in honor of the Passion, Resurrection, and Ascension of our Lord Jesus Christ, making remembrance also of the Blessed Virgin and all the saints, that they may intercede in heaven for us who strive to honor their memory here on earth.

Turning towards the people, he recommends them to pray that his sacrifice and theirs may be acceptable in the sight of the Almighty; after which he intones the "Preface" or introduction to the Canon of the Mass, calling upon those present to raise their hearts—"Sursum corda"—and join their praises of God with those of the nine choirs of angels, concluding with the "Sanctus" (Holy, Holy, Holy) in honor of the Blessed Trinity.

Then we come to

THE CANON OF THE MASS.

Canon is a Greek word meaning "rule," and is applied to this most solemn part of the Mass, which never changes, remaining substantially the same in all ages and liturgies.

It is always read by the priest in a very low voice, symbolizing the silence of our Saviour during the trials of His Passion.

A translation of the Canon is to be found in all English missals for the use of the laity.

The priest beseeches the Father of Mercies in behalf of the whole Church, the Pope, the bishop of the diocese, the Rulers of the country, and all orthodox believers. A commemoration is made for the living, for those in particular for whom the priest offers the Mass, making remembrance also of all present at the Sacrifice. A solemn commemoration is made of the saints in order to honor their memory and beg their intercession, after which the priest spreads his hands over the bread and wine, as the priests of old used to place their hands on the heads of the victims to be sacrificed to God (vide Book of Leviticus), begging of the Almighty to accept the offering made to Him, imploring His peace in this life, and eternal salvation in the next.

We then come to the very essence of the Mass, the

CONSECRATION,

when the priest makes use of the very words used by Christ Himself, pronounces them in His name with His power and authority, and thus changes the bread into the Body of Christ, and the wine into His Blood—the separate consecration of the sacred species constituting a mystic immolation.

The Sacred Host is then elevated, and after the Host the Chalice, in memory of Christ's elevation on the cross, and in order that all the faithful in the church may adore Jesus Christ there present with his Body and Soul, Humanity and Divinity, all under the sacramental veils. "As often as ye shall do these things, ye shall do them in memory of me."

After begging of God to accept the sacrifice from the hands of His High Priest, the priest makes a memento for the faithful departed, that they may obtain a place of refreshment, light, and peace through Christ our Lord—*per Christum Dominum nostrum*—all prayers in the Mass concluding precisely in the same manner, to testify our belief that it is only by virtue of His merits that we can obtain any favor whatsoever.

Then follows the "Pater Noster"—the Lord's Prayer—always read aloud or chanted, after which the celebrant says a prayer that we may be delivered from all evils, past, present, and to come, and, through the intercession of the Blessed Virgin and all the saints, be favored with peace in our days and secured from all sin and disturbance, through Christ our Lord.

The priest breaks the Host, in memory of Christ breaking bread before giving it to His disciples, and puts a particle in the chalice, to represent the reuniting of Christ's Body and Soul after the Resurrection, saying: "The peace of the Lord be always with you." He recites after this the "Agnus Dei" three times: "O

Lamb of God, who takest away the sins of the world, have mercy on us." Before consuming the Sacred Species, he says three more preparatory prayers and repeats the centurion's "Domine, non sum dignus"—"Lord, I am not worthy that thou shouldst enter under my roof; but only say the word, and my soul shall be healed."

After the Communion, the priest takes a little wine into the chalice (which we call the first ablution), in order to consume therewith whatever little drops of Sacred Blood may be adhering to the chalice, and the second ablutions of wine and water, for fear of any sacred particle, be it never so small, adhering to his fingers.

When a priest celebrates two Masses, he does not take any of the ablutions until the end of the second Mass, as a priest must be always absolutely fasting from midnight whenever he celebrates Mass.

After saying one or more prayers, he blesses all present—"May the Almighty God, the Father, the Son, and the Holy Ghost, bless you"—and generally concludes the Mass by reading the sublime beginning of the Gospel of St. John. Then all finishes by the acolytes saying, "Deo Gratias," in thanksgiving to God for all the graces received during the Holy Sacrifice.

The Mass is said in the

LATIN LANGUAGE,

as it is the ancient language of the Church. Moreover, it preserves uniformity of worship, and is not, like a living tongue, subject to change or corruption. Nor is this of any injury to the faithful, as they may always follow the priest, in the celebration of Mass, by making use of their missals or prayer-books; or, if they be unable to read, by meditating on the different stages of our Saviour's sufferings. Hence, no matter what part of the world a Catholic may travel, he is always at home, so to speak, in any Catholic church during the celebration of Mass.

Here I thought it would not be out of place to quote the beautiful sentiments of Johann Kaspar Lavater (a Protestant minister of Zurich, who died January 2, 1801) on finding himself in a Catholic church:

"He does not know Thee, O Jesus! who dishonors even Thy shadow. I honor all things where I find the intention of honoring Thee. What, then, do I behold here? What do I hear in this place? Does nothing under these majestic vaults speak to me of Thee? This cross, this golden image: is it not made for Thy honor? The censer which waves around the priest, the 'Gloria' sung in choirs, the peaceful light of the perpetual lamp, these lighted tapers—all is done for Thee? Why is the Host elevated if it be not to honor Thee, O Jesus! who hast died for love of us? Because it is no more bread, it is Thy Body, the believing church bends the knee. It is in Thy honor alone that these children, early instructed, make the sign of the cross, that their tongues sing Thy praise, and that they thrice strike their breasts with their little hands. It is for love of Thee, O Jesus! that one kisses the spot which bears Thy adorable Body, that the child who serves the altar sounds the little bell and performs all that he does. The riches collected from distant countries, the magnificence of chasubles—all that has relation to Thee. Why are the walls and the high altar of marble clothed with becoming tapestry on the day of the Blessed Sacrament? For whom do they make a road of flowers? For whom are all these banners embroidered? . . . Oh! delightful rapture for Thy disciples to trace the marks of Thy finger where the eyes of the world see them not. Oh! joy ineffable for souls devoted to Thee to behold in caves and rocks, in every crucifix placed upon the hills and on the highways, Thy seal and that of Thy love. Who will not rejoice in the honors of which Thou art the object and the soul?"

Such are the sentiments with which every Christian should be imbued on entering a Catholic church, more particularly when the Holy Mass is being celebrated. In this great Sacrifice we have a standing memorial of the Passion and Death of our Saviour, the fruits of which are applied to our souls. By means of these sacred mysteries we are kept united to Christ, and we render to the Almighty an unceasing, supreme act of worship.

"When we sacrifice," says the great St. Ambrose, "Christ is present, Christ is immolated."

Hence the splendor of our churches, the beauty of our vestments, the imposing grandeur of our ceremonies, the display of lights, the profusion of flowers, the religious awe and devotion of the people; all, all have in view the greater honor and glory of Jesus Christ, whom we believe to be truly and really present on our altars, the "Lord to whom belongs the earth and the fulness thereof."

II.

THE CONFESSIONAL.

THERE is no subject more uniformly or more persistently abused than the "Confessional." It has been a shining target for the shafts of ridicule as well as of calumny for the past three hundred and fifty years. There is now, and always has been during this long period of time, an immense amount of ignorance displayed whenever this important point of Catholic teaching has been discussed by those outside the Church.

With a considerable number of persons, especially in our time and in this country, the difficulty arises from a misunderstanding, or rather from want of proper knowledge on the subject. If, instead of reading the works of our enemies, who always misrepresent the Church and its doctrines, inquirers would consult some authorized Catholic work, or take in hand and read carefully, with unprejudiced mind, one of even those little catechisms to be found in possession of our Catholic children, much bitter and unjust prejudice would be removed, and we would be seen in our true light.

Now let us enter calmly and thoughtfully, like earnest men and Christians, into an examination of the "Confessional," the grounds on which it rests, the authority on which it is based, the wants and desires of the human heart which it so abundantly supplies and fulfils, the immense benefits it confers, not only on individuals in particular, but on society in general, and we shall learn to esteem it according to its true and perfect value.

Baptism, as is well known, washes away all sins from the soul, not only original sin, but also all actual sins previous to its reception, and remits the punishment due to the same. It makes a man a child of God and heir to the kingdom of heaven, and renders his soul pure and spotless in the sight of the Almighty. But as, unfortunately, the vast majority of those once purified in the saving waters fail to preserve in after-life their baptismal innocence, if there did not exist some other remedy, the human race would be in as sad a state as before. Our Blessed Saviour, knowing full well our poor, frail human nature, and that "man is prone to evil from his youth," in His infinite goodness and mercy instituted another sacrament—"a second plank of safety after shipwreck"—on which we may lay hold and be saved from everlasting ruin.

Our Divine Lord, as we learn from the 18th chapter of St. Matthew, after denouncing the sin of scandal and commanding that every incorrigible sinner should be reported to the Church; "and if he will not hear the Church, let him be to thee as a heathen and a publican," then and there conferred on His Apostles the divine power of binding and loosening: "Amen I say to you: whatsoever you shall bind upon earth, shall be bound also in heaven; and whatsoever you shall loose upon earth, shall be loosed also in heaven." He said the same to St. Peter in particular (ch. xvi. 18, 19). This wonderful power He conferred on the Apostles, and, in them, their successors, in still stronger terms after His glorious resurrection and ascension into heaven: "All power is given to Me in heaven and on earth" (St. Matt. xxviii. 18); or, as St. John expresses it (St. John xx. 21): "As the Father hath sent Me, I also send you. When He had said this, He breathed on them; and He said to them: Receive ye the Holy Ghost. Whose sins ye shall forgive, they are forgiven them; and whose sins ye shall retain, they are retained."

No human language could be plainer, clearer, or more expressive. The same wonderful power and godlike attributes received from His Heavenly Father, and possessed by Him as the Incarnate God, He bestowed on those who were to continue His work and govern His holy Church after His ascension, and until the end of time, when He would come again "to judge the living and the dead." The most wonderful and most divine of all these powers was that of absolving from sin: "Whose sins ye shall forgive, they are forgiven." This is their warrant, this their authority. It is impossible, absolutely impossible, to take any other meaning from the words of Christ, or to twist them to a contrary sense.

No one can doubt that Christ, as God, possessed this power; but we must bear in mind, and He Himself tells us most emphatically, that He possessed it also as the "Son of Man," when, in confirmation of this declaration, He worked a miracle on the paralytic: "And behold they brought to Him a man sick of the palsy, lying on a bed. And Jesus seeing their faith, said to the man sick of the palsy: 'Son, be of good heart, thy sins are forgiven thee.' And behold some of the Scribes and Pharisees said within themselves: 'This man blasphemeth.' And Jesus seeing their thoughts, said: 'Why do you think evil in your hearts? Which is easier to say, Thy sins are forgiven thee; or to say, Rise up and walk? But that you may know that the Son of man hath power on earth to forgive sins, then saith He to the man sick of the palsy: 'Rise up, take thy bed and walk.' And he rose up and went into his house. And the multitude seeing it, feared, and glorified God, who had given such power to men" (Matt. ix. 2-8).

Every one will admit that no man of himself has such power. No one can deny that God has it; and if God has it, is He not omnipotent, and cannot He delegate this power to whom He pleases? What sane man can refuse to believe it? Had not Christ the power of forgiving sins? and, if so, had He not the power also of delegating it? That He had this power and thus used it is evident from His own divine words already quoted, and which could not possibly be expressed in clearer terms: "And heaven and earth shall pass away before My words shall fail."

But some one may say: "Yes, it is true, we cannot deny it, the words are too clear; He conferred this power on the Apostles, but on no one else."

Ah, indeed! was the Church, then, to begin and end with the Apostles? Was there to be no salvation for the countless generations that were to come after them? What says Our Blessed Saviour? Surely *He* will give us the answer: "All power is given to Me in heaven and on earth. Go ye, therefore, teach all nations: baptizing them in the name of the Father, and of the Son, and of the Holy Ghost; teaching them to observe all things that I have commanded you: and behold I am with you all days, even unto the consummation of the world" (St. Matt. xxviii. 18–20). The Protestant version is precisely the same. The Apostles were not to live during all time; therefore what was said to them was evidently intended also for their successors in office, who were to continue the apostolic work of instructing all nations, tribes, and peoples. These were to have the same power, and to speak with the same authority, handed down in regular succession in that divine Church which Our Lord founded, with which He promised to remain during all time, directing, guiding, sustaining, and enlightening it, and against which He most solemnly declared "the gates of hell shall never prevail."

Such was the true, natural, and obvious sense in which Our Lord's words were accepted in His time by the Apostles and in every succeeding age by their successors, the Fathers and Doctors of the Church. As St. Paul said: "Let men so look upon us as the ministers of

Christ, and the dispensers of the mysteries of God" (1 Cor. iv. 1). And do we not read in the 19th chapter of the "Acts of the Apostles" that "many of those who believed came confessing and declaring their deeds"?

Consult the annals of the Church in every age from the very beginning of its history, and you will find the same belief as to the divinity of its institution.

If the people did not believe that it had been established by Christ Himself, they never would have received it, would never have submitted to such a yoke. If it be a human institution, *when, where,* and *by whom* was it invented? Surely these are very important questions, and such an event as its *invention,* did it ever happen, would have been altogether too important to have passed without notice—too important not to have left some trace behind it in the history of the times in which it was supposed to have taken place. But no such trace can be discovered.

What class of persons, moreover, could possibly have any interest in such an invention? Whom could it profit? The priests? Well, no, for many reasons.

1st. If the priests, bishops, or popes had been the inventors, they would certainly have contrived to exempt themselves from the painful and humiliating ordeal of confessing their own sins. Priests, bishops, and even popes, have to submit to the same law like the humblest and lowliest of their flock. The only difference is that they go to the holy tribunal more frequently than the members of the laity, as they stand in need of greater purity for the performance of their sacred functions.

2dly. It is the most painful, the most laborious, the most fatiguing of all the priests' duties, more especially in the larger parishes. But perhaps some very ignorant or very malicious person may say: "They get paid for it." A more diabolical falsehood was never uttered. Never, in the history of the Church, was it lawful to accept any money whatsoever for the hearing of confessions and the granting of absolution. It would be justly considered one of the most heinous crimes and sacrileges that could be committed, and would be visited by the heaviest penalties the Church could inflict. I never read or heard of such a case, and it is too ridiculous to treat seriously.

Suppose then that, at any given period of the history of the Church, the ecclesiastical authorities took it into their heads to establish the Confessional and then announced it to the body of the faithful; select any age you like, or a particular year in any century. Do you think that the people would ever have submitted to such a heavy burden, would willingly have subjected themselves to such a humiliating ordinance? Whoever does, has a far different idea of human nature than the most of intelligent persons.

Those who lived in the third, the sixth, the tenth, or the thirteenth century had the very same passions, as much human pride as the men of this nineteenth century, and would have been just as rebellious under what they would have believed to be an ecclesiastical imposition. Hence they would never have bowed down to such a law, did they not know and believe that it was established by Christ Himself.

Some individuals have gone so far as to say that the Confessional was established by the Church in the Fourth Council of Lateran, A.D. 1215, but that Council only fixed the limit of time beyond which it would be reckoned a grievous sin to neglect the Sacrament of Penance.

In the first ages of the Church, the piety and zeal of the faithful needed no spur to the performance of their duty in this respect, since they approached the Sacraments every day, or at least every week; but when the fervor of the people diminished and their charity grew cold, it was deemed necessary to establish the law of Confession and Communion, to be complied with at least once a year, and then at Easter or thereabout, under pain of excommunication.

That the Confessional existed from the time of Christ and His Apostles, the

TESTIMONIES OF THE FATHERS

and Doctors of the early Church, which I shall now quote, will clearly and amply demonstrate.

In the first few centuries of the Christian era, so great was the piety of the faithful that they generally made their confessions publicly and underwent public penance for their sins. This was the custom until thirty years after St. Augustine's time, when Pope Leo abolished it, for fear of scandal and disedification.

Let us begin with the twelfth century, and select a testimony here and there among the different ages until we reach the immediate disciples of the Apostles.

Pierre de Blois (who died A.D. 1200) thus speaks: "Let no one say to himself, I confess in secret and I do penance in the sight of God; if such a confession were sufficient, 'the keys' were in vain given to Peter. Does shame prevent you from confessing? If so, remember that your conscience will be exposed before all men in the day of judgment' (*Tract. de Conf. Sacram*).

The very essence of the Sacrament of Penance is given in very few words by Richard of St. Victor (died A.D. 1173): "Vera pœnitentia est abominatio peccati cum voto cavendi, confitendi, satisfaciendi"—having a horror for sin, with the resolution of being more watchful, making confession and rendering due satisfaction.

"Of what advantage is it," says the great St. Bernard, "to declare but a certain number of your sins and to conceal the remainder? All things are naked and open to the eyes of God, and how dare you conceal anything from Him who holds the place of God in so great a sacrament?"

"Non salvemini nisi confiteamini"—you will not be saved unless you confess—says Hugo of St. Victor.

St. Anselm, who was Archbishop of Canterbury in the beginning of the twelfth century, declares that "we should go to the priests and beg absolution." The great Doctor of the Church, St. Peter Damian, says that "to be ashamed of confessing our sins is to fear God less than man."

"We have observed," declared the Fathers of the Second Council of Châlons, A.D. 813, "something which needs to be corrected, namely, that certain individuals in making their confession do not do so with necessary integrity. They should examine their sins with care and attention in order that it should be full and entire."

The Venerable Bede, who flourished in the beginning of the eighth century in England, thus discourses: "We should distinguish between slight faults and sins of more weight; as to the former, we may usefully confess them before our equals in order to obtain their prayers and receive correction; but as for the latter, in order to fulfil the law, we should necessarily confess them to the priest."

FATHER CONFESSORS IN THE EARLY AGES.

St. Viron was confessor to King Pepin; St. Aidan, to King Brandubh; St. Martin, a monk of Corbia, to the great Charles Martel; St. Aldric, Bishop of Mans, to Louis le Débonnaire; St. Udalric, Bishop of Augsburg, to the Emperor Otho; and Arteldulf, prior of St. Oswald, to Henry I. of England.

Charlemagne made it a rule that every regiment should have its father confessor.

William of Somerset, a monk of Malmesbury, praises the Normans for having spent the night before battle in confessing their sins.

A council held in Kent, A.D. 787, forbade prayers to be said for those who, through their own fault, died without confessing their sins.

"Let each one prove himself," says St. Paulinus (eighth century), "before receiving the Body and Blood of Jesus Christ. Before approaching let us have recourse, as is our duty, to confession and penance; let us examine with care all our works, and if we remark in ourselves whatever is capable of causing us to abstain from receiving, let us hasten to remove it by confession and true penance, for fear that, like Judas the traitor, harboring the devil within us, we may perish."

Lactantius declares that "That is to be known as the true church in which are to be found confession and penance."

Alcuin, the preceptor of the Emperor Charlemagne, wrote a work against the heretics of his time who denied the necessity of confession.

Tertullian, who lived in the age following that of the Apostles, says, in his great work *De Pœnitentia:*

"I think that many decline confessing their faults, or delay it from day to day, more moved by fear of shame than care of their salvation; like unto those who, afflicted with secret diseases, conceal their malady from the physicians, and perish from false modesty and bashfulness. What advantage can be derived from the hiding of our crime; for if we succeed in having it escape the knowledge of men, can we conceal it from God?"

That man of wonderful learning, Origen, says: "We must have recourse to confession in order that we may be freed from our sins" (Second Homily on Thirty-seventh Psalm).

St. Basil (who died in the year 378) gives a similar testimony: "We should confess to those to whom the dispensation of the mysteries of God is accredited."

It is related in the life of St. Ambrose that when he heard the confessions of his penitents, he wept so much over the recital of their sins as to cause themselves to weep. We shall conclude these testimonies by the declarations of the two great Doctors of the Church, St. Augustine and St. John Chrysostom, the former the greatest light of the Western, as the other was of the Eastern Church: "Let no one say," says St. Augustine, "that 'I do penance in private and in the sight of God. God who pardons me knows the sorrow of my heart.' Was it therefore said in vain: 'Whatsoever ye shall bind upon earth shall be bound also in heaven'? Were the keys given in vain to the Church of God? Shall we render fruitless the Gospel of God and the words of Christ?" (Hom. 49).

"God granted unto the priests of the New Law," says St. Chrysostom, in his work "De Sacerdotio," "what was never granted to angels or archangels, for never was it said to them, 'Whatsoever ye shall bind on earth shall be bound also in heaven.'"

So we perceive very clearly what ample proof we find in the Sacred Scriptures and in the writings of the fathers of the Church for the Catholic doctrine of the Confessional. We see also from the very words of the divine commission, "Whose sins ye shall forgive, they are forgiven them, and whose sins ye shall retain, they are retained," that the power thus conferred is a discretionary one, not, therefore, to be exercised according to the whim, fancy, or caprice of its possessors, but according to prudence and judgment.

How may this be done? By no other possible way than through the Confessional; for the case of each one must be carefully examined, his sins and the number of them, their gravity, their malice, the character and dispositions of the penitent; and then, and only then, is judgment to be pronounced.

THE PRIEST IN THE CONFESSIONAL

is a spiritual judge and spiritual physician. No judge worthy of the name will ever pass sentence without examining the whole case in all its bearings; so the priest must make himself, as much as possible, acquainted with his penitent, his passions, his inclinations, the causes of his fall, and all this under the seal of the most inviolable secrecy.

He is also a spiritual physician. No good physician will prescribe for his patient without making a proper *diagnosis*, or, in other words, without knowing clearly what is the disease, how far it has developed, what are all the symptoms, what remedies it is necessary to order, what diet and what mode of living he should counsel. So, likewise, the penitent should make known to his spiritual adviser the state of his soul, its hidden sores, its weaknesses, its failings and perverse inclinations, in order that he may receive such counsel and advice as will be necessary or beneficial for the welfare of his immortal soul.

Even if God and his Church had not ordered it, nature itself would seem to demand the institution of such a tribunal. When the poor, weary, overburdened heart feels itself oppressed, it instinctively seeks for an outlet to its grief and sorrow in some such channel as is thoughtfully prescribed by Holy Mother Church.

How beautifully and truthfully is this great need of the human heart portrayed in

HAWTHORNE'S "MARBLE FAUN,"

where the heroine of his story, after suffering untold anguish, is irresistibly impelled, Protestant though she be, to enter a confessional box in St. Peter's Church, Rome, and there unburden herself of the terrible secret that was eating into her very life.

"THE WORLD'S CATHEDRAL.

"Gliding onward, Hilda now looked up into the dome, where the sunshine came through the western windows and threw across long shafts of light. They rested upon the mosaic figures of two evangelists above the cornice. These great beams of radiance, traversing what seemed the empty space, were made visible in misty glory by the holy cloud of incense, else unseen, which had risen into the middle dome. It was to Hilda as if she beheld the worship of the priest and people ascending heavenward, purified from its alloy of earth, and acquiring celestial substance in the golden atmosphere to which it aspired. She wondered if angels did not sometimes hover within the dome, and show themselves, in brief glimpses, floating amid the sunshine and the glorified vapor, to those who devoutly worshipped on the pavement.

"She had now come into the southern transept. Around this portion of the church are ranged a number of confessionals. They are small tabernacles of carved wood, with a closet for the priest in the centre; and, on either side, a space for a penitent to kneel, and breathe his confession through a perforated auricle into the good father's ear. Observing this arrangement, though already familiar to her, our poor Hilda was anew impressed with the infinite convenience —if we may use so poor a phrase—of the Catholic religion to its devout believers.

"Who, in truth, that considers the matter, can resist a similar impression? In the hottest fever-fit of life they can always find, ready for their need, a cool, quiet, beautiful place of worship. They may enter its sacred precincts at any hour, leaving the fret and trouble of the world behind them, and purifying themselves with a touch of holy water at the threshold. In the calm interior, fragrant of rich and soothing incense, they may hold converse with some saint, their awful, kindly friend. And, most precious privilege of all, whatever perplexity, sorrow, guilt, may weigh upon their souls, they can fling down the dark burden at the foot of the Cross, and go forth to sin no more, nor be any longer disquieted; but to live again in the freshness and elasticity of innocence.

'Do not these inestimable advantages,' thought Hilda, 'or some of them, at least, belong to Christianity itself? Are they not a part of the blessings which the system was meant to bestow upon mankind? Can the faith in which I was born and bred be perfect, if it leave a weak girl like me to wander, desolate, with this great trouble crushing me down?' A poignant anguish thrilled within her breast; it was like a thing that had life, and was struggling to get out. . . . In this vast and hospitable cathedral, worthy to be the religious heart of the whole world, there was room for all nations; there was access to the Divine Grace for every Christian soul; there was an ear for what the overburdened heart might have to murmur, speak in what native tongue it would. When

Hilda had almost completed the circuit of the transept, she came to a Confessional—the central part was closed, but a mystic rod protruded from it, indicating the presence of a priest within, on which was inscribed: 'PRO ANGLICA LINGUA.' It was the word in season! If she had heard her mother's voice from within the tabernacle calling her, in her own mother-tongue, to come and lay her poor head in her lap, and sob out all her troubles, Hilda could not have responded with a more inevitable obedience. She did not think, she only felt. Within her heart was a great need. Close at hand, within the veil of the Confessional, was the relief. She flung herself down in the penitent's place, and, tremulously, passionately, with sobs, tears, and the turbulent overflow of emotion too long repressed, she poured out the dark story which had infused its poison into her innocent life. . . . And, ah, what a relief! When the hysteric gasp, the strife between words and sobs, had subsided, what a torture had passed away from her soul! It was all gone; her bosom was as pure now as in her childhood."

No Catholic could give a more perfect picture than this of the natural longing of the human heart for such a divine institution as the Confessional.

Count De Maistre, speaking on the same subject, says: "The stomach which contains poison and which throws itself into a convulsion in order to reject it, is the natural image of a heart into which crime has poured its venom. It suffers, it labors, it contracts itself until it reaches the ear of friendship, or at least that of benevolence."

How beautifully and faithfully the Holy Church of God accommodates itself to the wants and desires of the human soul, no want being left unsatisfied, no desire unfulfilled. Gifted with the divine wisdom of its Holy Founder, it comes to our rescue in every difficulty, it provides a remedy for every disease of the soul; it is a source of strength for every weakness, and of comfort for every sorrow. It has none but words of cheer in all our sadness and discouragement, and advice and consolation in all our trials and temptations. It has a salve for every hidden sore, a soothing balm for every affliction, a refreshing bath of soul-cleansing waters in the holy Sacrament of Penance.

In this Sacrament, besides Confession, there are two other essential parts, namely, contrition and satisfaction.

Contrition is a sincere, deep, and heartfelt sorrow for all our sins, because they are displeasing to God, who is infinitely good in Himself and infinitely good to us; and, moreover, because by them we lose all right to heaven and deserve eternal punishment. This sorrow necessarily includes a firm purpose of amendment. Without this sorrow or contrition no absolution pronounced by a priest is of any value whatsoever. So necessary is it, that not even God Himself can dispense us from this requisite disposition.

When the sorrow is perfect, or proceeds from the pure love of God, and is joined with the expressed or implied desire of sacramental absolution, it justifies the sinner immediately. Such has always been the teaching of the Church, as may be clearly seen from the decrees of the Œcumenical Council of Trent, session 14, ch. iv.

Besides contrition, the other requisite quality is satisfaction. Hence, if any injury have been done to any one in character, person, or property, full reparation must be made to the entire extent of the penitent's ability. If the penitent be in unjust possession of any property whatsoever, there is no forgiveness, and no hope of it, until that property be restored to its rightful owner. Even were the confessor deceived in such a case, so as to give absolution, it would be *absolutely null and void.* Nor would it suffice to give the property or its equivalent in charity or for any pious object, if the real owner were known or could be easily discovered. Restitution should then be made to him and to him only —to satisfy the law.

God alone knows the countless restitutions that have been made through the Confessional, the innumerable reparations effected, the causes of scandal removed, private enmities overcome, revenge subdued and heinous crimes prevented.

It is the great guardian of the morals of the youth of both sexes. Rising passions are checked or kept under control, and vice is nipped in the bud. Innocence is preserved from many fatal snares, or, if it have been unfortunately lost, the penitent is saved from despair and headlong ruin and restored to God's grace and friendship. The young man is warned on the very threshold of life, the young woman is rescued from the proximate occasion of sin, and the dangers of a sinful life are pointed out to all.

Preaching from the altar or pulpit has not and cannot have the same powerful effect as the word spoken in season, and whispered into the ear of the individual penitent by the Minister of God in the sacred tribunal. That is the place for special warnings and instructions adapted to the widely different wants, dangers, and necessities of the penitents. There the means are pointed out and the remedies prescribed for the prevention or cure of the maladies of the soul.

"I look upon a pious, earnest, and discreet confessor," says the eminent Protestant writer Leibnitz, "as a great instrument in the hands of God for the salvation of souls; for his counsels serve to direct our affections, to enlighten us as to our faults, to help us avoid occasions of sin, to dissipate doubts, to raise the downcast spirit—in fact, to remove or mitigate all diseases of the soul; and if we can hardly find anything on earth more excellent than a faithful friend, what happiness to find one who shall be bound by the inviolable religion of a divine Sacrament to preserve the faith and to succor souls."

Never yet, in the long history of the Church, has there been found one case, well authenticated, of the seal of the Confessional having been violated. Priests have fallen from grace and even abandoned the faith; but no matter how low they have fallen, they were never yet known to reveal the secrets of the Confessional. A priest can never make any use whatever—to the slightest detriment of the penitent—of any revelation made to him through the sacred tribunal. No law, human or divine, can oblige him to make the slightest disclosure.

St. John Nepomucene suffered a glorious martyrdom, and is thereby honored on our altars, because he would not make known to the king the confession of his spouse the queen. He preferred a cruel death to the violation of the sacred seal.

The very infidels themselves are forced to give their testimony in favor of the Confessional. Voltaire says: "It is a divine institution, which has had its origin only in the infinite mercy of its Author" (tome xxxiv. page 36). He said, moreover, that "the enemies of the Roman Church, who have opposed so beneficial an institution, have taken from man the greatest restraint that can be put on crime" (*Dict. Phil.*, art. "Catechisme de Curé").

"A well-informed man," says Gibbon, "cannot resist the weight of historical evidence which goes to establish that confession was one of the principal points of papist doctrine in all the period of the four first centuries."

Lord Fitzwilliam (*Letters of Atticus*) says that "it is impossible to establish virtue, justice, and morality on a solid basis without the tribunal of penance."

Now let us give the testimony of one of our own, the truly Catholic Eugénie de Guérin, from her famous Journal: "The world does not know what a confessor is to one: the man who is a friend of the soul, its most intimate confidant, its physician, its master, its light; he who binds and looses, who gives us peace, who opens the gates of heaven; to whom we speak upon our knees, calling him as we do God, our father; nay, faith makes him in very deed God and Father to us. When I am at his feet, I see in him only Jesus Christ listening to the Magdalen and forgiving her much because she has loved much."

It is said in the Divine Book that *"there is joy before the angels of God over one sinner doing penance."* How the angels of God then must cluster around the Confessional, watching with eager joy their precious charges emerge from the holy tribunal with happiness beaming on their countenances and "a peace that surpasseth all understanding" filling their minds and hearts to overflowing, with those words of divine cheer ringing in their ears, the words of God's own sacred minister to each penitent soul: " Beloved child, thy sins are forgiven thee. Go in peace and sin no more."

III.

THE INTERCESSION OF SAINTS.

THE most consoling of all the doctrines of the Catholic Church is the Communion of Saints. How perfect the accord, how grand the harmony, of the whole system of dogma! No discord, no jarring, no contradiction, but a complete nexus between all the parts of the divine whole—a marvellous unity and a perfect chain of connected truths.

What a grand and sublime idea we cannot but form of the Church—one body of which Christ Our Lord is the Head, and all its members in their different states joined together by the bonds of an unbroken, undying charity!

How deeply affecting and powerfully encouraging is the thought and the belief that our present course in this weary, sinful world, is being momentarily watched by the blessed spirits, who reign with God in the heavens above; that they take the deepest interest in our eternal welfare, more especially those disembodied spirits of "the just made perfect" who once passed through the same struggles on earth; that they pray for us and intercede for us with the good God! How we also, weak, frail mortals that we are, can be of help to others, more particularly to those who departed this life in the friendship of the Almighty, and who are not yet sufficiently purified to enter the "Holy of Holies," where nothing the least defiled can gain access, as we are told by St. John in the Apocalypse.

Behold, then, the bond—the wonderful, divine bond of charity, which unites us all, whether in heaven above, the earth beneath, or the expiatory prison-house of purgatory.

I shall now endeavor to explain one part of this admirable communion—that is, the relations existing between us and the Saints of God; the foundations upon what this pure and consoling belief rests, and the wonderful advantages it confers on the faithful Christian.

After some preliminary remarks, we shall see what warrant there is for this dogma in the Sacred Scriptures.

The chief idea of this doctrine is that the Saints of God, being purer and holier than we, and having attained their eternal happiness in an everlasting union with the Almighty, we believe that their prayers on our behalf are more pleasing and acceptable in His sight than our own poor, unaided petitions can expect to be.

The clear, unmistakable words of the Church itself on this subject, in the celebrated Council of Trent, leave nothing to be desired as to the meaning of the dogma:

"It is good to consider," says Bossuet (in his *Exposition of Catholic Faith*), "the words of the Council itself, which, wishing to prescribe to bishops how they should speak of the 'Intercession of Saints,' obliges them to teach that 'the Saints who reign with Jesus Christ offer to God their prayers for men; that it is good and useful to invoke them in a suppliant manner, and to have recourse to their aid and succor, in order to beseech God for His favors, through His Son Jesus Christ, who alone is our Saviour and Redeemer.'" *Per Filium ejus Jesum Christum Dominum Nostrum, qui solus noster Redemptor et Salvator est:* these are the very words of the Council, than which nothing can be plainer or clearer, or farther from the idea of idolatry or superstition.

No injury is done to the Creator, there is no derogation from His laws, no abridgment of His rights, in the honor and reverence we pay the Holy Ones of God.

SUPREME WORSHIP

is due to God alone, and to offer it to any creature, no matter howsoever elevated, be it to the highest of the Seraphim or to the Mother of God herself, would be the fearful crime of idolatry.

We adore God alone, as He is the Author of life, the Creator of all things, the Supreme Master, Director, and Governor of the universe. We adore not the Angels, we adore not the Saints, we adore not the Virgin Mother. We never offer the Sacrifice of the Mass to them, but to the Eternal, Living, and True God—"Æterno Deo, vivo et vero." Mass may be said, and is often said, in honor of the Saints, but is never offered to them.

In reverencing them, in paying them a certain limited homage or worship, we but reverence the very gifts of God Himself. Whatever they have or possess in the way of virtue, grace, or glory they have received from Him who is "the Giver of every good and perfect gift."

In praising the saints we honor the very creations of God. "Mirabilis Deus in sanctis suis"—"God is wonderful in his saints," says the Psalmist. They are His friends—"I call you no more servants, but friends"; they are His intimates. They "fought the good fight" in His cause here, they triumphed over the world, over the evil ones in high places, and over their evil passions, with the help of God's grace; now their salvation is secure, now their labors are rewarded; they have already received their crown, and now they glory in the presence of their Lord and their God. They have no longer any anxiety for their own souls' salvation, but they take the deepest interest in ours; they are ever ready to help and assist us, and to beseech the Almighty in our behalf.

Nor is it displeasing to Him, but, on the contrary, most agreeable in His sight, that we should invoke their aid.

The Almighty, as a rule, never seems to work directly either in the natural or the supernatural world. He ordains or permits, as the cases may require, secondary agents to carry out His designs. He has His ministering spirits, His angels, His messengers, constantly accomplishing, throughout the whole universe, His most merciful and beneficent designs.

As in the natural order, so also in the supernatural—we all depend on one another for mutual aid, assistance, and support. Each one has his appointed work to do; as in the human frame all the members form but one body, and though each has its own function to perform yet they are mutually dependent. This is beautifully described by St. Paul in his First Epistle to the Corinthians (ch. xii. 14–30).

There is a hierarchy in heaven, there is a hierarchy on earth. There are different orders having different offices, and a mutual dependence existing between them.

How many persons there are whose salvation and sanctification may depend, to a considerable extent, on our prayers and good example! How much we ourselves owe to others for the many graces we have received we shall never know until we stand before God's tribunal.

"There are many things," says the great St. Augustine, "which God does not grant without a mediator and intercessor." The Almighty has so willed it; it is the order of His Divine Providence, to which we are all subject, and we know and believe that "He doth all things well."

If we consult the Old as well as the New Testament, we shall find ample proofs of this doctrine.

In the Book of Genesis (ch. xx. 7) we read that God warned Abimelech, King of Gerara, that he was to obtain his pardon only through the intercession of Abraham—"He shall pray for thee, and thou shalt live."

When God was about to destroy the people of Israel on account of their idolatry they were saved only through the prayers of Moses (Exodus xxxii.)

The friends of Job could only obtain pardon after he should pray for them. "Go to my servant Job, and offer for yourselves a holocaust, and my servant Job shall pray for you; his face I will accept, that folly be not imputed to you" (Job xlii. 8).

The angel who appeared to Josue (v. 14) said that he was "The prince of the host of the Lord," and commanded him to loose the shoes from off his feet, which Josue did, falling on his face and worshipping him, as the Scriptures declare. ("Fell on his face and did worship," according to the Protestant version.) Of course it was not divine worship, but that kind of inferior worship or homage which we Catholics pay to the angels and saints.

The blessed spirits are ministers and counsellors of God. "Thousands of thousands ministered unto Him; and ten thousand times a hundred thousand stood before Him" (Daniel vii. 10). "All the army of heaven standing by Him on the right hand and on the left" (xxii. 19).

Cities, provinces, and kingdoms are placed under their guardianship and protection. "The prince of the kingdom of the Persians resisted me one-and-twenty days; and behold Michael, one of the chief princes, came to help me," said the angel to the prophet Daniel (x. 13). "I will tell you what is set down in the scripture of truth, and none is my helper in all these things but Michael, your prince" (verse 21). St. Michael has always been considered as the Guardian Angel of the Church of God.

St. Paul declares that the Lord Jesus "shall come to be glorified in His saints, and to be made wonderful in all them that have believed" (2 Thess. i. 10). Our Blessed Saviour said to His Apostles that "all those who followed him in the regeneration, when the Son of man shall sit on the seat of His majesty, shall sit on twelve seats judging the twelve tribes of Israel" (Matt. xix. 28).

The angel Raphael declared to Tobias (xii. 12) that he was the spirit who offered his prayers and good works to the Almighty.

St. John gives the following testimony in the Apocalypse: "Another angel came and stood before the altar, having a golden censer; and there was given to him much incense, that he should offer of the prayers of all saints upon the golden altar, which is before the throne of God. And the smoke of the incense of the prayers of the saints ascended up before God, from the hand of the angel" (viii. 3, 4).

The Apostle St. James tells us (ch. v) that "the continual prayer of a just man availeth much," and we have proofs of it in the cases already cited of Abraham, Moses, and Job. If their prayers availed much when they were here upon earth, how much more so now that they are in an immeasurably closer union with God in the land of the blessed! If asking the intercession of saints be injurious to God and the infinite merits of Christ, much more so would it be to ask the prayers or beg the intercession of our fellow-men on earth, poor, miserable sinners like ourselves, or, if they be just men, certainly liable at any time to lose their justice; and yet St. Paul disdained not, time after time, to ask the prayers of his fellow-Christians: "I beseech you, therefore, brethren, through our Lord Jesus Christ, and by the charity of the Holy Ghost, that you assist me in your prayers for me to God" (Romans xv. 30).

The Book of Ecclesiasticus, from the forty-fourth to the fiftieth chapters inclusively, is filled with the praises of the saints.

See also the fifteenth chapter of the Second Book of Machabees, wherein it is related that Onias the high-priest and Jeremias the prophet appeared in a vision to Judas Machabeus. "Now the vision was in this manner: Onias, who had been high-priest, a good and virtuous man, modest in his looks, gentle in his manners, and graceful in his speech, and exercised from a child in all virtues, holding up his hands, prayed for all the people of the Jews. After this there appeared also another man, admirable for age and glory, and environed with great beauty and majesty. Then Onias answering, said: This is a lover of his brethren, and of the people of Israel: this is he that prayeth much for the people, and for all the holy city, Jeremias the prophet of God."

Thus the sacred Scriptures afford a solid foundation for the reverence we pay to the saints and the utility of invoking their intercession.

We have the testimonies also of the Holy Fathers showing

THE BELIEF AND PRACTICE OF THE EARLY CHURCH,

and proving, moreover, how the Almighty favored this doctrine, by most wonderful miracles, attested and authenticated by irreproachable witnesses, by some of the greatest lights that ever appeared above the horizon of this earth—men who were noted no less for their profound erudition and vast acquirements than for their wonderful holiness and apostolic virtues.

The language which they used is much stronger than ours in reference to the power of intercession of the saints and the deep reverence to be paid their relics. If we are to be accused of idolatry, much more so may they be accused of the same, and we would then be obliged to come to the conclusion that our Blessed Saviour had scarcely left the earth before that Church, which He promised to sustain until the end of time against all the assaults of hell, fell into an idolatry as deep as that in which the Gentiles were plunged before His advent.

The holy Fathers believed, exactly as we do now, that whatever honor, whatever reverence, whatever worship, in its more restricted sense, was paid to the saints redounded to God's greater glory —that His honor suffered no diminution, that confidence in Jesus Christ and His infinite merits was by no means lessened or impaired, but, on the contrary, increased, as the saints could never have merited were it not for the Sacrifice of Calvary.

Let us give a glance at the testimonies of the Fathers from the very dawn of Christianity, and we shall see that the teaching of the Catholic Church has never varied on this important point of doctrine.

St. Polycarp, the first bishop of Smyrna, was a disciple of St. John the Evangelist, the cherished apostle of the Lord. We find the account of his martyrdom related in the Epistle of the Church of Smyrna to the Church of Pontus, and contained in the history of Eusebius, who is called the "Father of Ecclesiastical History." We there read that Polycarp having been sentenced to be burned, the flames, by a miracle of God, suspended their activity in his regard; whereupon the executioner, becoming impatient, plunged his sword into the body of the martyr, whose blood rushed out in such a stream as to extinguish the fire. For fear that the Christians might take away his body and worship it, as the governor was told by the Jews who were present, he ordered it to be reduced to ashes, and there were left but a few remnants of the bones, which the faithful gathered with the greatest reverence and with far greater care than if they had been gold and precious stones—"Gemmis pretiosissimis cariora et quovis auro potiora." Removing the remains to a proper place, where they were reverently deposited, the faithful assembled there every year to celebrate with every demonstration of joy—"cum hilaritate et gaudio"—the anniversary of the glorious martyr (lib. iv. *Hist. Eccl.* cap. 15.) We there see devotion to the saints, veneration of relics, celebration of feast-days, the same in the very first age of the Church as we behold now in the nineteenth century.

The same author relates the conversion and martyrdom of St. Basilides, which took place in his own age (the third century). Basilides was one of the pagan guards who led St. Potimiana to martyrdom, and having, on the way to the place of execution, shielded her from insult, she promised him that after her death she would beg of God a reward for his kind service. Three days after her martyrdom she appeared before him, placing a crown upon his head and informing him that the Almighty heard her prayer on his behalf. Whereupon, finding himself suddenly converted, he asked for instruction, embraced the faith, and shortly afterwards obtained the crown of martyrdom.

The great St. Cyprian, Bishop of Carthage, made an agreement with Pope Cornelius that whoever of them should die first would intercede for the other and help him by his prayers. In his work *De Virginibus* he beseeches the holy virgins, that when they reach the next life and obtain their reward, not to be unmindful of him in their prayers.

St. Gregory Nazianzen relates of St. Justina, who was a virgin and martyr in the third century, that, in order to overcome a terrible temptation arising from some diabolical influence brought to bear against her virtue by a young pagan enamored of her beauty, she had recourse to the Virgin Mary, and by prayer and fasting was thereby delivered through her intercession from the well-nigh fatal snare.

St. Basil, the most exact of all the Greek theologians of the early ages, in his profession of faith addressed to the Emperor Julian the Apostate, says:

"I acknowledge the holy apostles, prophets, and martyrs, and I invoke them in order that they may pray for me to God, and by their intercession obtain his mercy for me." In his homily on the forty martyrs he thus speaks: "He who is weighed down with anguish flies to them, he who is in joy also has recourse to them; the former that he may be freed from his sorrow, and the latter that he may be all the more established in his prosperity. Here may be found the mother praying for her children and the wife begging for the safe return and good health of her husband."

What was deemed not only innocent but even salutary by the fervent Christians of the second, third, and fourth centuries cannot with reason be condemned in the nineteenth. The great saints and doctors whom I quote did not introduce these pious customs, but found them already existing in the Church. "Be mindful," says St. Basil in his thirty-sixth homily, "of the holy martyr Memmas, whom many of you now present have found a helper in your needs, bringing you success in serious difficulties, ensuring a safe return, restoration to health, or even the raising to life of some of your children already dead—"Filios jam mortuos ad vitam reductos reddidit."

St. Gregory of Nysse appeals to the martyr St. Theodore: "It is to your intercession that we owe our present tranquillity; be our protection likewise in the future. If more powerful advocacy be necessary for us, call on all your brother martyrs, solicit Peter, persuade Paul, prevail on John, the Beloved Disciple, not to forget the churches which they established with so much labor and suffering."

St. Cyril of Jerusalem (who died A.D. 386) speaks of the custom that prevailed in the East: "When we offer the Holy Sacrifice we make remembrance of those who have gone before us—first the patriarchs, then the apostles and the martyrs—in order that God, moved by their prayers, would hear ours more favorably."

"Obsecrandi sunt angeli, obsecrandi sunt martyres"—"We should beseech the angels, we should beseech the martyrs," says the eloquent St. Ambrose.

The learned St. Jerome wrote an entire work against Vigilantius, who opposed the doctrine of invocation of saints.

St. John Chrysostom declares that not only in Rome, but also in his own capital at the East, kings and emperors considered it an honor to be buried in the very vestibules of those churches where reposed the bones of the martyrs and apostles, so satisfied were they to become, as it were, "the very doorkeepers of the fishermen"—"Fiantque piscatorum ostiarii reges."

A very ample testimony as to this important doctrine, given by the great St. Augustine, may be found in the eighth chapter of the twenty-second book of his most celebrated work, *The City of God.* As it would be too long to quote, I shall merely give here an extract from his writings on the Gospel of St. John (86th tract.): "At the Lord's Table we do not make mention of the martyrs, as we do of others who rest in peace, to pray for them, but rather that they should pray for us"—"Sed magis ut orent pro nobis." In this short quotation we find mention of two important doctrines—namely, the invocation of saints, and prayers for the dead.

Prudentius, the great Latin poet of the Christian era, wrote a beautiful poem on the vast concourse of people that were accustomed to visit the tomb of St. Hippolyte; the rich and the poor, the patricians as well as the peasants, blocking up the very roads in their anxiety to venerate the martyr's remains, and in search of health for soul and body through his intercession:

"Hic corruptelis animique et corporis æger,
 Oravi quoties stratus, opem ferui."

In every age the greatest reverence was paid to the

RELICS OF THE SAINTS,

more particularly to those of the martyrs. Their bones, the ashes of their bones, or their blood carefully preserved in vials or sponges, were all treasured up by the early Christians, and esteemed beyond all price.

We see innumerable instances of this in the writings of the Fathers, and I have already quoted the account given by the Father of Ecclesiastical History of the special homage paid to the remains of the blessed martyr Polycarp, who was a disciple of St. John the Evangelist.

St. John Chrysostom relates, in a letter to his sister Marcellina, the great respect and reverence paid to the relics of the holy martyr St. Ignatius (who was bishop of Antioch about one hundred years after our Saviour's time) when his remains were brought back, in glorious triumph, from Rome, and honored with the highest marks of veneration as they were carried through the various cities *en route* to their destined resting-place.

The Sacred Scriptures teach us what reverence is due to the relics of the holy ones of God; for do we not read in the 4th Book* of Kings (ch. xiii. 21) how a dead man was raised suddenly and unexpectedly to life when his body was cast into a grave where reposed the remains of the great prophet? "And

---

* 2d Book of Kings according to the Protestant version.

some that were burying a man, saw the rovers, and cast the body into the sepulchre of Eliseus. And when it had touched the bones of Eliseus, the man came to life, and stood upon his feet." How powerful are the relics of a great saint!

The same is proved from the Acts of the Apostles xix. 11, 12: "And God wrought special miracles by the hand of Paul. So that even there were brought from his body to the sick *handkerchiefs* and *aprons*, and the diseases departed from them, and the wicked spirits went out of them." Nothing can be clearer; and if we did not find this testimony in Holy Writ it would be looked upon, by those outside the Church, as the most degraded kind of superstition to believe that miracles could ever be wrought by the "handkerchiefs" and "aprons" of St. Paul, or of any other saint in the calendar. A number of people were healed of their infirmities, and unclean spirits were expelled by the very "shadow" of Peter, the Prince of the Apostles (Acts v. 15, 16).

As it is closely connected with the subject of relics, a few words on

IMAGES

may not be out of place. They were not absolutely forbidden in the Old Law, for God Himself gave orders for some to be made—for instance, the figures of the Cherubim that were to be placed on each side of the Mercy-Seat in the Sanctuary (Exodus xxxvii.), and by divine ordinance also in the Temple of Solomon (1 Paral. xxviii.)

What was forbidden was to make any graven thing so as to make an idol of it, or to worship it.

The Catholic Church teaches, and commands pastors to teach, that there is no inherent virtue in statues or images by which they can hear or help us, and that we are not to expect any aid from them—all of which would be gross idolatry.

Any respect or reverence we pay to them is only a relative honor, and is referred to their prototypes, or the beings represented by them. We venerate the cross, but whatever homage we pay it is intended for the person of Jesus Christ Himself. When we bow before a statue it is not to the lifeless statue we offer any reverence, but to the living Saint in heaven whom it was meant to represent.

How sovereignly reasonable, then, is devotion to the Saints! how strongly supported by Holy Scripture and by the testimonies of the brightest and best Christians of all ages since the time of Christ!

How eminently consoling and encouraging is such a belief! What a happy feeling it engenders in our hearts to think and to know that, no matter how poor, how miserable, or how forsaken we may be in this life, how sorely tempted or oppressed with fear and sadness, that there are

BLESSED SPIRITS

hovering near us, that they take the deepest interest in our well-being, that they are ever ready to help and assist us by their prayers and intercession, and to lead us in the paths of truth and righteousness!

How instructive, also, when we propose them to ourselves as models for imitation!—knowing full well that there was no station in life, from the humblest to the most exalted, which they did not adorn with the highest Christian virtues; that they had the same, and even greater, difficulties than we to overcome; they had the same trials and temptations to undergo, the same passions to subdue, and the same real yet invisible enemies to war against—the powers of darkness in the high places.

"That which we have seen and heard we declare unto you, that you may have fellowship with us, and our fellowship may be with the Father, and with His

Son, Jesus Christ" (1 John i. 3). This is the fellowship or

SWEET COMMUNION

of which I speak, and in which we all believe. "Giving thanks," says St. Paul, "to God the Father, who hath made us worthy to be partakers of the lot of the saints in light" (Colossians i. 12).

St. Augustine says that "the honor rendered to heroes is the best encouragement to heroism"; so I may say with equal truth that the honor rendered to Saints is the best encouragement to sanctity.

Whether we live in a kingdom or a republic, we cherish the memories of the great men who flourished before our time, especially those who were of lasting service to their country, who successfully fought its battles, who did honor to its name, who spread its reputation abroad, who conferred benefits on society by their great learning, their useful inventions, their warlike genius, their statesmanlike qualities, or by their notable benefactions to the whole community.

We hold their memories in veneration, we erect statues in their honor, and we cherish with peculiar pride and affection whatever relics they have left behind, in order to remind a grateful posterity of their noble lives.

What American worthy of the name can recall the memory of Washington without feelings of affection, and even reverence? And how dearly he would prize even the slightest memento of the Father of his Country! What fond mother but presses to her heart the portrait of a long-lost, beloved son—preserving, with the deep reverence of motherly affection, the smallest token of that life that has gone out from her; of that light which is extinguished; of that flower which has withered away in its fair young morn of existence?

These are the feelings and instincts of the human heart, and we do but transfer them to that life still dearer to us—still more real as it is also more spiritual—the life of the soul and everything that tends to render more vivid the great truths of the supernatural order.

Not only the unlettered, the poor and the ignorant, need these helps to devotion, which supply the place of books and sermons; but let a man be never so intellectual or well instructed, and, if he be possessed of any Christian faith or feeling, the vivid representation, on wood or on canvas, of his crucified Redeemer will often have more effect in moving his heart and soul than the most polished writing or studied discourse.

Our holy Church is a most tender and affectionate Mother. She knows all the wants of our nature, and most effectively does she supply them, raising our souls to God, attracting them from the things of earth to bid us fix our gaze on something higher, something holier, something far more worthy of our sighs and labors—the Heavenly Jerusalem, towards which we should always tend, knowing that "here we have no lasting city, but we seek one for to come."

IV.

DEVOTION TO MARY.

DEVOTION TO MARY BEGAN AT THE FOOT OF THE CROSS ON CALVARY.

THE grand work for which the Divine Word, the Second Person of the Adorable Trinity, came down from heaven and became incarnate, was now near its full and complete accomplishment. But a few moments yet remained before His visible presence should be withdrawn from the earth, before the Sun of eternal justice should set, and set with a most bloody setting.

The terrible drama of Calvary was drawing to a close. The material sun of our world was preparing to hide itself at the approach of the most awe-inspiring event that ever happened in the universe, at which all nature felt the terrible shock. The reckless, cruel, sight-seeing multitude were on their way back to the city of Jerusalem, satiated, as they were, with the scene of blood they had that day witnessed. A small band of soldiers remained on guard, whilst the faithful few lingered on Calvary's mount.

The Sacrifice was well nigh complete. The Saviour was nailed to the Cross, and was hanging in dreadful agony. His treasure of Sacred Blood was fast oozing away, and His cup of bitterness and desolation was being rapidly drained. He had offered up His life for the salvation of men, and in a few moments more all would be consummated.

Our Lord had one more legacy to bequeath—a legacy most precious, a legacy most dear to His Divine Heart, of which the world was not worthy; but His charity knew no limits. But one member of the apostolic band was present at the Crucifixion, and he was the Beloved Disciple—the virginal apostle, John the Evangelist. To him, then, as the representative of all the faithful, Our Saviour left the most precious legacy He had then to bestow—His own dear

VIRGIN MOTHER,

the Mother of Sorrows—*Mater Dolorosa*—standing there, in mute agony, at the foot of the Cross: "Son, behold thy Mother; Mother, behold thy son."

By the death of Jesus on the Cross we became His brethren, adopted children of His Heavenly Father, and co-heirs with

Him of the eternal kingdom. Giving us God for our Father, He made His Mother our Mother also, wishing us to be like unto Himself in all things, so far as it is possible for creatures so to be.

All devotion to Mary, all the teaching of the Catholic Church with regard to her dignity, her prerogatives, her power—all springs from the incarnation of Our Lord, the sacred pivot on which all history, whether sacred or profane, must turn; all events—the rise and fall of kingdoms, the spread of literature, the progress of science, the advancement of civilization—all revolving around that one grand central point of the moral universe.

To understand the Incarnation as it is, as the Catholic Church understands it and wishes it be understood, is to have the key to the whole edifice of Christian dogmas. When we have a clear and exact idea of it, all doctrines having any reference to the Blessed Virgin, the inconceivable dignity to which she was raised, the astonishing height of virtue and sanctity which she attained, and her wonderful power of intercession, which are but its natural consequences —all become perfectly clear and intelligible.

In this mystery of the Incarnation we believe that the Second Person of the ever-adorable Trinity, the perfect image of God the Father's infinite beauty and sovereign excellence, and the infinitely perfect expression of His uncreated wisdom and intelligence, in the fulness of time descended to this earth in order to assume our human nature, to become man, to take unto Himself a human soul and a human body.

He descended, in order that we might ascend. He condescended to our infirmity, in order that we might rise to His higher life and happiness. The end which God had in view, in the Incarnation of the Word, was the deification of the creature—that man might be elevated to a supernatural order of existence and participate in His own divine life and beatitude.

The great instrument, chosen by God from all eternity to carry out His most holy design, was the Virgin Mary. What a destiny! A creature to bring forth a Creator, a servant her Lord, the redeemed one her Redeemer! How favored and peculiarly blessed beyond the countless millions of maidens that ever inhabited or ever should dwell upon the earth! How pure, how holy, how perfect must she have been! The Almighty must have showered His most special graces and favors upon her, in order to make her a worthy recipient of such an honor.

No other created being was ever so holy, ever so perfect. Always free from every fault and imperfection, not the slightest shadow of sin ever flitted over her soul. Purest, loveliest of virgins, humblest of maidens, given to retirement, rapt in contemplation, constantly engaged in prayer, object of delight to the whole heavenly court, she remains for evermore the most privileged, most blessed, most glorified of God's creatures. She was perfect in every virtue, unrivalled in purity, incomparable in innocence. Such was the one destined in the eternal counsels to be the Mother of the God-Man.

What dignity in the universe, outside the Godhead, can compare with Mary's? Conceive all that is grand and sublime in creation; let fancy take its flight on angelic wings beyond the confines of the earth; let man be gifted with the deepest and most luminous intelligence of the brightest of the Seraphim, and he could not possibly imagine anything greater or more sublime than to be the Mother of Jesus!

It would be impossible, absolutely impossible! The Almighty could not bestow on any created being any dignity to surpass it, for no one can attain to anything higher than to be the Mother of the Incarnate God.

No one ever reached before, no one ever shall reach again, the dignity with which Mary has been blessed—a position and dignity that shall remain for ever. As Jesus was born and Jesus died, never to be born, never to die again, so no other created being shall ever have the same claim on Him as to be called His Mother. She alone rejoices in that most beautiful of titles, that grandest of dignities—

THE MOTHER OF JESUS.

This it is that elevates her above the whole world, above the entire universe—next to God Himself—far above the patriarchs and prophets, the virgins and confessors, the martyrs and apostles, and even far above the Angels and Archangels, the Powers and Dominations, the

Cherubim and Seraphim, as the Queen-Mother of the Kingdom of Heaven.

The chief cause, then, of all her glory, the source of all her sanctity, the origin of all her power, is the divine maternity. "That man cannot be right at heart," says Dr. Nevin, a Protestant divine, "in regard to the faith of the Incarnation, whose tongue falters in pronouncing Mary the Mother of God."

We call her, and justly, the "Mother of God"; and here is how we reason, according to the clear, syllogistic form, than which nothing can be more forcible:

Jesus Christ is God; but Mary is the Mother of Jesus Christ; therefore Mary is the Mother of God.

The premises are perfectly plain, intelligible, and undeniable to any one who believes in the divinity of Christ; that the conclusion naturally follows no logician can deny.

We do not say that Mary was the Mother of the divinity in Christ, no more than we say that such a woman was the mother of such a child's soul. Man is composed of body and soul, both of which are necessary to the formation of him as a man. We all know, when we speak of a woman being the mother of such a one, that she did not create his soul, which God alone could do; yet we say with perfect truth she is the mother of such a person. The body and soul do not form two distinct personalities, but one simply. So, also, there are two distinct natures in Jesus Christ, the divine and the human, but there is only one personality. If there were two persons in Christ (which would be heresy to admit), then we should say that Mary is the mother of the human and not of the divine person. But this is absolutely untrue, for the Divine Word, in assuming a human body and a human soul — in other words, becoming man and a perfect man—retained His own personality and did not assume another. He whom we call Jesus Christ is really and truly God as well as man—not two persons, but one person with two natures hypostatically joined. Hence, Mary being the Mother of Jesus, and Jesus being God, Mary becomes *ipso facto* Mother of God. This is her title by just right, and it is consequently no sign of idolatry to give her this appellation. Nestorius, who denied it to her, was solemnly condemned by the Fathers of the Church in solemn council assembled at Ephesus A.D. 431.

When the Divine Word left His heavenly throne—the bosom of the Eternal Father—to take flesh in the womb of Mary and to become man, He did not assume our nature merely for a time, say thirty-three years, and then cast it off for ever. No; having assumed it once, and having really become perfect man as he was already true God, for ever afterwards, and during the never-ending ages of eternity, human nature remains as truly His nature as the divine. He has made it his own, and He will preserve it as such—immortal, glorious, and impassible—at the right hand of the Eternal Father, where He, the God-Man, shall never cease to be the source of endless delight to the whole court of heaven.

His Sacred Humanity, all of which He received from the pure, untainted blood of the blessed Virgin Mary, and in which He suffered unto death—a death most cruel for the sins of men—that Sacred Humanity shall shine with a splendor and a glory that would cast millions of suns far more brilliant than ours into an ignominious shade, and His Sacred Wounds shall send out for ever a light which countless firmaments could not possibly equal.

Too many are apt to forget the sublime part of

MARY IN THE REDEMPTION.

and the honor and glory which of right belong to her in consequence. Let such persons take the Bible, and ponder over its sacred words in relation to the mystery of the Incarnation—that great mystery hidden in the bosom of God from all eternity, revealed to the patriarchs, announced hundreds of years in advance by the prophets, the object of the desires, prayers, and sighs of countless millions from the fall of Adam.

To whom was it announced, and by whom was it to be accomplished? Not to any of the great ones of the earth, its lords or princes, its literati, scientists, or philosophers, but to a poor and humble Virgin of Nazareth. "The weak ones of this world doth God choose that He might confound the strong."

Wonderful to relate, the Almighty condescends so much as to ask the consent of this humble and unknown maiden. Yes, in the wonderful order of Divine Providence, the *consent* of Mary was necessary for the accomplishment of the great mystery of the Incarnation (St. Luke i. 27–35). The Almighty commissions one of His highest messengers —the Archangel Gabriel—to announce this wonderful mystery to Mary, and to inform her that she is the instrument chosen by God for its accomplishment.

The angel salutes her with the deepest reverence: "Hail, full of grace! the Lord is with thee. Blessed art thou among women." She, in her great humility and spotless virginity, was troubled at his saying; but he still further assured her: "Fear not, Mary: for thou hast found grace with God. Behold, thou shalt conceive in thy womb, and shalt bring forth a son, and thou shalt call his name Jesus."

Not yet was she fully assured; for,

from her most tender years, she had vowed her virginity to God, and this priceless treasure not even for the most exalted of dignities was she willing to lose or renounce. "How shall this be done, since I know not man?" Most wonderful of miracles, in the omnipotence of God she was to preserve her virginity and yet become a mother, as was foretold, eight centuries before, by the prophet Isaias: "Behold, a virgin shall conceive and bring forth a Son, and they shall call his name Emmanuel, which, being interpreted, is, God with us."

"The Holy Ghost," says the Archangel announcing the coming miracle to her, "shall come upon thee, and the power of the Most High shall overshadow thee, and therefore also the Holy One that shall be born of thee shall be called the Son of God." Then it was that Mary gave her consent to the Incarnation of the Divine Word in her womb, and the consequent redemption of the human race: "Behold the handmaid of the Lord: may it be done to me according to thy word"—Ecce ancilla Domini: fiat mihi secundum verbum tuum.

Shortly after Mary visited her cousin, St. Elizabeth, and at the very sound of Mary's voice John the Baptist leaped for joy in his mother's womb: "And Elizabeth was filled with the Holy Ghost, and said: 'Blessed art thou among women, and blessed is the fruit of thy womb'" (exactly as Catholics have been repeating ever since, and, since the Holy Ghost inspired it, they certainly cannot and should not be condemned for following His inspiration). Elizabeth then continues: "And whence is this to me, that the mother of my Lord should come to me?" (The same words are to be found in the Protestant as well as the Catholic version of the Scriptures.)

Why, then, object to us for styling Mary, as St. Elizabeth did whilst acting under an inspiration of the Holy Spirit, "the Mother of my Lord"? Wherein lies the difference, "the Mother of the Lord" or "the Mother of God"?

If Mary be Mother of the Lord, she is the Mother of God. If Jesus Christ is God, Mary, then, is Mother of God.

The late Rev. Dr. Wm. Faber, one of the loveliest characters that ever lived, had a great devotion to Mary, and wrote the following poem in her honor while he was a member of the Episcopal Church of England:

MARY.

"But scornful men have boldly said
    Thy love was leading me from God;
And yet in this I did but tread
    The very path my Saviour trod.

"They know but little of thy worth
    Who speak these heartless words to me;
For what did Jesus love on earth
    One-half so tenderly as thee?

"Get me the grace to love thee more;
    Jesus will give, if thou wilt plead;
And, Mother, when life's cares are o'er,
    Oh! I shall love thee then indeed.

"Jesus, when his three hours were run,
    Bequeathed thee from the Cross to me;
And, oh! how can I love thy Son,
    Sweet Mother, if I love not thee?"

Well indeed might Mary exclaim, after hearing the inspired words of St. Elizabeth: "Behold, from henceforth all generations shall call me blessed." Generation after generation have since appeared upon the earth, millions upon millions of mortals — differing in race, education, manners, and dispositions—and they have vied in honoring her name and extolling her virtues.

Wherever Jesus was adored in spirit and in truth, there likewise was reverenced His Holy Mother. The Fathers and Doctors of the Church in every age have published her praises and the power of her intercession. Kingdoms and provinces were placed under her protection, and countless millions felt the salutary influence of her life and example. Well indeed might she give utterance to that prophetic declaration: "From henceforth ALL generations shall call me blessed"; for blessed, in truth, she is, by reason of her exalted sanctity, her sublime prerogatives, and her great glory in the Church of God.

The Almighty, destining Mary to be the Mother of the Incarnate Word, destined her likewise for the possession of all those graces and virtues, and that eminent sanctity, so necessary to support with becoming fitness this most exalted of dignities. Hence we believe that no human mind, not even an angelic intelligence, can conceive an adequate idea of the unsurpassable height of holiness which she has reached.

It is only natural to suppose that a loving son would do all in his power to show his affection for the mother that bore him. Consider, then, such a Son and such a Mother! Having it in His power—a power to which there is no limit—He must have absolutely lavished His gifts and graces on Mary.

The first of these gifts and graces, in the order of time, was her

IMMACULATE CONCEPTION,

whereby she was preserved, by the preventing grace of the Redeemer, in the very first instant of her existence in her mother's womb, from the stain of original sin. Had it never been proclaimed by the infallible Church, I, for one, cannot see the slightest shadow of a difficulty in believing such a dogma, but, on the contrary, far more difficulty in the other hypothesis. For it would seem a disgrace to our Blessed Saviour, and the host of hell might taunt Him with it for all eternity, if ever, even for one instant, Mary, His Mother, had been in the power of Satan—and such undoubtedly would have been the case had she been stained with the taint of original sin.

Hence the honor of the Incarnate God demanded her exemption, and His Own infinite merits purchased it for her. Mary, of herself, could not possibly merit such a favor, such a privilege. It was accorded to her only in view of Christ's merits. She owes her redemption to Him, as well as do other Christians, but there is this difference: in her case it was a preventing grace—that is, a grace going before, according to the original meaning of the word *prevent;* in our case it is subsequent. It would have been altogether unbecoming in her, whom the Divine Word chose for His Mother, to have been thus stained.

Impressed with a like idea, the charming poet Wordsworth, though not of the Catholic Faith, thus expresses it:

> " Mother! whose virgin bosom was uncrossed
> With the least shade of thought to sin allied;
> Woman! above all women glorified,
> *Our tainted nature's solitary boast;*
> Purer than foam on central ocean tost,
> Brighter than eastern skies at daybreak strewn
> With fancied roses, than the unblemished moon
> Before her wane begins on heav'n's blue coast,
> Thy image falls to earth. Yet some, I ween,
> Not unforgiven, the suppliant knee might bend
> As to a visible power, in which did blend
> All that was mixed and reconciled in thee
> Of Mother's love with maiden purity,
> Of high with low, celestial with serene."

Whatever honors were conferred upon her, whatever privileges and graces—and they were exceedingly great—were all granted on account of her Divine Son, to make her, in so much as any created being could be made, a worthy Mother of such a Son.

Is it surprising, then, that we should

venerate her whom the Eternal Father has so exalted as to choose her for His adopted daughter, whom the Divine Word selected for His Mother, whom the Holy Spirit made His own spouse? "Thou art all fair, my dove, and there is no stain in thee" (Canticle of Canticles).

All the homage we render to her redounds to the greater glory of God, and more especially to the glory of that Sacred Humanity of Our Lord Jesus Christ which He took whole and entire from her pure, spotless, untainted flesh and blood.

To invoke her

INTERCESSION

is, therefore, not displeasing to God, is no derogation from the divine worship due to Him, nor, in any way, prejudicial to His Divine Mediatorship.

We believe that Christ is the sole Mediator between His Heavenly Father and us, our sole Redeemer, our Lord and our God. But we believe also, as I explained in the foregoing treatise, that it is in the order of His Divine Providence, that it is His wish, His desire, that we should beg the intercession of His faithful servants, of those near and dear to Him on account of their long-tried fidelity and approved sanctity. We believe, and we oftentimes even feel, that the blessed ones of God hear us, watch over us and sympathize with us, for does not the Gospel teach us that "there shall be joy before the angels of God over one sinner doing penance." Our Blessed Lord, moreover, assures us that His saints, His chosen ones, shall be like the angels in the kingdom of heaven.

The greater the sanctity the nearer to God; the nearer to God the more powerful the intercession. As St. Paul assures us, there is a glory of the sun, and a glory of the moon, and a glory of the stars, and "star differeth from star in glory." Among all beatified spirits Mary stands pre-eminent, as she is pre-eminent in holiness and pre-eminent in dignity.

If asking her intercession or that of the other saints be a reflection on the divine Mediatorship of Christ, with at least as much reason is the practice of asking the prayers of one another upon earth. What earnest, sincere Protestant who sends his note of petition to his minister in the pulpit, asking his prayers and those of the congregation, ever thinks that he is thereby offering an insult to the Mediatorship of the Saviour? His action in such a case is but a natural consequence of the principle which we advocate.

Do we not read in the Gospel how some of the Gentiles, desirous of an audience with our Blessed Saviour, did not go directly to Him, but laid their petition before Philip, because he was one of the Apostles; and Philip addressed himself to Andrew, whom he believed to be deeper in the confidence of Our Lord? What is this if not intercession?

Who, then, can estimate, with anything like an approximation to the truth, the wonderful and well-nigh unbounded influence which Mary has with her Divine

Son? Did ever son love a mother as Jesus Christ, the God-Man, loved His spotless Mother? Never; and the brightest angel in the kingdom of heaven shall never be able, during all eternity, to fathom the intensity of that affection. His will and hers formed but one on earth; they form but one now in heaven.

Did she ever refuse Him anything while He was subject to her upon earth, and can He refuse her anything she asks of Him now that they are joined together in the kingdom of His glory?

Mary gave Him every particle of His Sacred Flesh and Blood; she suckled Him in infancy, she guarded His infant footsteps, she watched over His youth, she fondly gazed on His opening manhood; she saw herself in His features that caused

Him to be everywhere recognized as *her* Son; she was the first to behold Him on His entrance into this world, the last to linger by His Cross and to receive His last sigh. How powerful, then, must be her influence over His Divine Heart!

Search Holy Writ and you will there find sufficient proof of the power of her intercession. Read attentively the Gospel of St John with regard to the marriage feast of Cana in Galilee (John ii. 1-11). It is easy to perceive that it was through her intercession that Our Blessed Saviour, although declaring that His time had not yet come, worked the great miracle of changing water into wine. This was His very first miracle and public manifestation of His divine power.

Our adversaries quote some of the

words contained in this relation as not being over-respectful on the part of Christ to His Mother, *v. g.*: "Woman, what is that to Me and to thee? My hour is not yet come."

There is an old axiom which reads, " Quod nimis probat, nihil probat"—What proves too much, proves nothing. If, by the Scriptural words just quoted, you prove that Christ was disrespectful to His Mother, then surely He was not the divine person we believe Him to be; for did he not, as God, lay down the commandment in the Old Law, "Honor thy father and thy mother"; and do you think He would afterwards give us an example in direct violation of His own command—He who declared that He came to fulfil the entire Law, and not to disregard it?

The *tone of voice* in which He uttered the words in question would change the meaning very materially; and if we go back to the original language in which they were uttered—the Chaldaic—they have a totally different signification: "Man bain anta uni ana"—There is but one thought between us.

Leaving the words, however, as they stand, and their meaning is to be judged from the context. If Our Blessed Saviour thought that His Mother's request was presumptuous or ill-timed, He certainly would not have granted it. After those words of supposed rebuke, what does the sacred text tell us? That His Blessed Mother undoubtedly knew the issue, is evident from what she said to the waiters: "Whatever He shall say to you, do ye." Whereupon He Himself gave orders to the waiters to fill the water-pots with water, to draw out and carry them to the chief steward, who, on tasting, found it to be the best of wine. "This beginning of miracles did Jesus in Cana of Galilee," at the request of His Holy Mother and through her special intercession, although there did not seem to exist any necessity for such a display of His power, more especially since He Himself declared that "His time had not yet come." *Facts* speak louder than *words*. He waived all these reasons in favor of Mary, and thus "manifested His glory, and His disciples believed in Him." This

FIRST MIRACLE,

worked in honor of Mary, the Mother of God, and through her special intercession, was but the beginning of that series of miraculous events which have since transpired in the world, and have been witnessed and authenticated by trustworthy, competent witnesses, in every age of the Christian era.

"Her maternal charity," says Bossuet, "having contributed so powerfully to our salvation, in the mystery of the Incarnation, which is the principle of all grace, she will contribute thereto eternally in all the other operations which are its dependencies."

The greater devotion we have to Mary, the more shall we love her Son; the more reverence we pay to her, the deeper shall be our adoration of the God-Man. One leads to the other infallibly; were it otherwise, then devotion to Mary would be condemnable. As the great

Bossuet—the Eagle of Meaux—declared, "Toute notre dévotion pour la Sainte Vierge est inutile et superstitieuse, si elle ne nous conduit à Dieu"—All our devotion to the Blessed Virgin is useless and superstitious if it conduct us not to God, in order that we may possess Him eternally and enjoy our heavenly inheritance.

Or, as St. Francis de Sales, the most amiable of men, says: "He who is anxious to please God and Our Blessed Lady does well, very well indeed; but he who would wish to please Our Lady as much as or more than God would be guilty of an unpardonable disorder."

All her glory, all her virtue, all her wonderful sanctity and well-nigh boundless power, she has received from her Divine Son, and by reason of His infinite merits. Nor is He jealous of any honor we pay her; as well might it be said that the sun is jealous of the moon which shines with his reflected light.

The strangest and most unaccountable fact that I have ever noticed in religious differences is, that good, honest, and sincere persons, outside the Catholic Church, pay due reverence to the memories of the special friends and intimates of Our Lord—His disciples and apostles, to Martha, Mary, Lazarus, and even Mary Magdalen; to Sts. Peter, James, and John the Beloved Disciple (although I must say that they are sometimes chary of their praises of St. Peter), and yet, *mirabile dictu!* they withhold the slightest veneration and, so to speak, even the most common civilities from her who was undoubtedly elevated above all others, and who was the nearest and dearest to Our Divine Lord.

I have read hundreds of sermons, preached by ministers of different denominations, and yet not in one of every hundred have I seen the name of Mary mentioned. The very name of Mary, the Mother of Jesus, instead of inspiring the deepest respect and love, seems to shock them, so that it would appear that they are in constant dread lest, if they were to utter it with the slightest mark of respect, they would be immediately condemned as Papists and Mariolatrists.

Not of this class is Oliver Wendell Holmes, who, although not a Catholic, yet beautifully speaks of that name:

"Is thy name Mary, maiden fair?
 Such should, methinks, its music be,
 The sweetest name that mortals bear
 Were best befitting thee;
 And she to whom it once was given,
 Was half of earth and half of heaven."

I believe that many are hardly to blame for the sad and unfortunate sentiments which they hold, so deeply have they been imbued, from their earliest childhood, with the most unfounded and even ridiculous

PREJUDICES AGAINST THE CATHOLIC CHURCH,

and all its doctrines, accusing us of idolatry, superstition, and kindred abominations, which we detest and abhor as much as, and even more than, they do.

The late Dr. Orestes Brownson, a convert to the Faith, and one of the deepest and most powerful minds America ever produced, thus expresses himself on this subject:

"We can well remember the time when our belief in the slanders against Catholics, forged in the heart of the Reformation, and handed down unimpaired to our day, was as implicit and religious as it was in the denunciations of our Lord against the Scribes and Pharisees. We had drawn these things from the very breasts of our mother. They were mingled with our first ideas; were articles in our infant creed. As we grew up we had no more doubt of their truth than we had of the events of Redemption. And we remember, too, what astonishment we felt when a suspicion of their falseness had forced itself upon us; and how when this suspicion expanded into clear conviction our faith was shaken in almost everything, how we trembled lest upon examination we should find the traditions in favor of Christianity itself as baseless as we had found those against Catholicity; and it was only through an interposition of the great mercy of God that we did not fall a victim to the scepticism thus produced, so firmly had these poisonous roots of false tradition entwined themselves with the earliest shoots of our belief in essential truth. Our experience teaches us a lesson of Christian sympathy and forbearance. It furnishes to our minds a plain reason, and almost an excuse, for that which often appears unaccountable, if not criminal, to old Catholics. They, having always enjoyed the light, cannot comprehend how Protestants should mistake it for darkness; or mistake the nature of things which it freely reveals. But to us who have seen things from the Protestant point of view this is by no means wonderful. We can well understand how people in the dark should commit blunders, how if a man walk in the night he stumbleth, 'because there is no light in him.'"

An unbiassed meditation on many passages of their own version of the Scriptures, or a calm and unprejudiced perusal of the simplest Catholic Catechism, would remove many of their strongest objections.

There is one thing certain: No one can really adore Jesus Christ "in spirit and in truth," and not love and reverence His Blessed Mother. Any dishonor or insult to her must necessarily rebound on Him. On leaving the earth, the scene of His labors, the most precious legacy, after that of His own most Precious Blood, which He bestowed upon the world was His own pure, Immaculate Virgin Mother, to whom we may fly in time of need, whose succor we should ask in time of danger, under whose protection we should place ourselves and all our interests, in order that she might lead us, by her powerful intercession, safely and surely to the feet of Jesus—"the way, the truth, and the life."

When Columbus, a good and faithful Catholic, discovered America he named the first island on which he set foot San Salvador, in honor of our Redeemer. (The English, who came afterwards, looking upon this as a mark of superstition, changed the name to "Cat Island.") The second island he discovered he named in honor of the Immaculate Conception of Mary: Santa

Maria de la Concepcion. The vessel in which he sailed for the new world was called the "Santa Maria."

The town of St. Augustine, Florida, forty years older than any other in the United States, according to Bancroft, was founded on the Feast of the Nativity of the Blessed Virgin, after the celebration of a High Mass in her honor.

The Chesapeake Bay was first called St. Mary's. Father James Marquette, the Jesuit, who first explored the Mississippi to the mouth of the Arkansas, called it the Immaculate Conception A.D. 1673, one hundred and eighty-one years therefore, before it was proclaimed as a dogma, which shows that it was not a new doctrine, but one always believed in the Catholic Church.

Montreal, founded over two hundred

and forty years ago, was first called Ville-Marie—City of Mary. In November, 1653, Father Chamount erected the first Catholic Church in the State of New York, and called it St. Mary's.

Thus it is easy to perceive that devotion to the Blessed Virgin is not new even in this country, placed as it is by our prelates under the patronage of the Immaculate Conception. So we may truly say, in the beautiful words of our gifted American poet, Longfellow:

> " This is the Blessed Mary's land,
> Virgin and Mother of our dear Redeemer.
> All hearts are touched and softened at her name ;
> Alike the bandit with the bloody hand,
> The priest, the prince, the scholar, and the peasant ;
> The man of deeds, the visionary dreamer,
> Pay homage to her as one e'er present.
> And e'en as children who have much offended
> A too indulgent father, in great shame, penitent
> And yet not daring unattended

To go into his presence, at the gate
Speak with their sister, and confiding wait
Till she goes in before and intercedes :
So men, repenting of their evil deeds,
And yet not venturing rashly to draw near
With their requests an angry father's ear,
Offer to her their prayers and their confession,
And she for them in heaven makes intercession.
And if our faith had given us nothing more
Than this example of all womanhood,
So mild, so merciful, so strong, so good,
So patient, peaceful, loyal, loving, pure,
This were enough to prove it higher and truer
Than all the creeds the world had known before."
—*The Golden Legend.*

V.

PURGATORY.

PURGATORY is a state of suffering for such souls as have left this life in the friendship of God, but who are not sufficiently purified to enter the kingdom of heaven—having to undergo some temporal punishment for their lighter sins and imperfections, or for their grievous sins the eternal guilt of which has been remitted. In other words, we believe that the souls of all who depart this life—not wicked enough to be condemned to hell, nor yet pure enough to enjoy the Beatific Vision of God—are sent to a place of purgation, where, in the crucible of suffering, the lighter stains of their souls are thoroughly removed, and they themselves are gradually prepared to enter the Holy of Holies—where nothing defiled is permitted to approach.

Jesus Christ, we doubt not, made satisfaction for all by offering Himself a willing victim on Calvary's mount to appease the offended majesty of the Deity; otherwise heaven would remain for ever closed against all the children of men Though this sacrifice was offered for all, yet it does not avail unto their salvation unless each individual co-operate with the grace and mercy of God, and unite his efforts, feeble though they be, with the labors and sufferings of Our Blessed Saviour.

The Almighty will not save us in spite of ourselves, or without our hearty concurrence. Hence, we must make use of the means which He so generously provides for the earnest working out of our eternal welfare. These means are the Sacraments of His Holy Church—instituted by Jesus Christ Himself for the purpose of conveying grace to our souls.

As we have already seen, in the treatise on the Confessional, we may obtain pardon of all our sins—committed after baptism—in the tribunal of Penance if we have true sorrow for our evil deeds and a firm purpose of amendment, if we humbly confess our transgressions, and receive the absolution of the priest, who stands in the place of God and is vested with His authority. The eternal guilt is then washed away, and the eternal punishment due to mortal sin is remitted; but there generally remains some *temporal* pains to be undergone, either in this life or the next.

Moreover, there are many

VENIAL FAULTS

which the majority of persons commit (such as anger, vanity, "white lies," etc.), and for which they have little or no sorrow—sins which do not deprive the soul of God's friendship, and yet are displeasing to His infinite holiness. For all these we must suffer either in this life or the next. Divine justice weighs everything in a strict balance, and there is no sin that we commit but for which we shall have to make due reparation. Faults which we deem of little or no account the Almighty will not pass unnoticed or unpunished. Our Blessed Saviour warns us that even for "every idle word that man shall say he shall render an account in the day of judgment."

We know full well that no man will be sent to hell merely for an "idle word" or for any venial fault he may commit; consequently there must be a place where such sins are punished. If they be not satisfied for here upon earth by suffering, affliction, or voluntary penance, there must be a place in the other life where proper satisfaction is to be made. That place cannot be either heaven or hell. It cannot be heaven, for no suffering, no pain, no torment is to be found there, where "God shall wipe away all tears from their eyes, where death shall be no more, nor mourning nor weeping." It cannot be hell, where only the souls of those who have died enemies of God are condemned to eternal misery, for "out of hell there is no redemption."

There then must be

A MIDDLE PLACE

where lighter faults are cleansed from the soul and proper satisfaction is rendered for the temporal punishment that still remains due. The punishment of every one will vary according to his desert. Our Blessed Saviour, according to the Gospel of St. Luke (chapter xii. 40-48), mentions different grades of punishment for sinners—those whose portion shall be appointed "with unbelievers," those who "shall be beaten with many stripes," and others "with few stripes."

Here is the text in full:

"Be ye then also ready, for at what hour you think not, the Son of Man will come.

And Peter said to Him: Lord, dost thou speak this parable to us or likewise to all? And the Lord said: Who (thinkest thou) is the faithful and wise steward, whom his lord setteth over his family, to give them their measure of wheat in due season? Blessed is that servant, whom when his lord shall come, he shall find so doing. Verily, I say to you, he will set him over all that he possesseth. But if that servant shall say in his heart: My lord is long a-coming, and shall begin to strike the men-servants and maid-servants, and to eat and drink and be drunk: the lord of that servant will come in a day that he expecteth not, and at an hour that he knoweth not, and shall separate him, and shall appoint him his portion with unbelievers. And that servant who knew the will of his lord, and hath not prepared.

and did not according to his will, shall be beaten with many stripes. But he that knew not, and did things worthy of stripes, shall be beaten with few stripes."

Our Divine Lord warns us to make necessary reparation whilst we have the time and opportunity:

"Make an agreement with thy adversary quickly whilst thou art in the way with him; lest, perhaps, the adversary deliver thee to the judge, and the judge deliver thee to the officer, and thou be cast into prison. Amen I say to thee, thou shalt not go out from thence till thou pay the last farthing" (St. Matthew v. 25, 26).

This expresses the doctrine of purgatory most admirably. The Scriptures always describe our life as a pilgrimage. We are only on our way. We have to meet the claims of divine justice here before being called to the tribunal of the everlasting Judge; otherwise, even should we die in His friendship and yet have left these claims not entirely satisfied, we shall be cast into the prison of purgatory: And "Amen I say unto thee that thou shalt not go out from thence until thou pay the last farthing."

Mortal sin destroys the image of God in the soul, severs the bond of friendship that connects it with the Creator, and totally effaces every trace of divine beauty imprinted on it by the sanctifying grace of the Holy Spirit. This sin, moreover, renders the soul subject to eternal punishment and misery. Venial sin does not destroy sanctifying grace, deprives us not of the friendship of God, but it displeases Him, disfigures the beauty of the soul, and leaves upon it stains from which it must be purified before enjoying the immediate presence of God: "There shall not enter into it anything defiled" (Apoc. xxi. 27).

When a soul leaves this world with true and perfect sorrow for all past sins, whether light or grievous, being thus united to God by perfect charity, it has no purgatory to undergo, but is immediately admitted to the enjoyment of its eternal reward. Considering, however, human nature as it is, we have sufficient reason to think that there are few so blessed; yet there are many whom we consider good, faithful Christians and who are nevertheless stained with light sins and imperfections, for which they shall have to do penance here or hereafter. Nor is it unreasonable to suppose that there are many such who depart this life without sufficient sorrow or due satisfaction being made for these delinquencies.

Our Saviour declares (St. Matt. xii. 32) that "whoever shall speak a word against the Son of Man, it shall be forgiven him; but he that shall speak against the Holy Ghost, it shall not be forgiven him, either in this life or in the world to come"; which shows, as St. Augustine says in the twenty-first book of his work, "The City of God," that there are some sins (venial, of course) which shall be forgiven in the next world and that consequently there is a middle state or place of purgation in the other life, since no one can enter heaven having any stain of sin, and surely no one can obtain forgiveness in hell.

The testimony of St. Paul is very clear on this point of doctrine: "For no man can lay another foundation, but that which is laid; which is Jesus Christ. Now if any man build on that foundation, gold, silver, precious stones, wood, hay, stubble: every man's work shall be made manifest; for the day of the Lord shall declare it, because it shall be revealed by fire; and the fire shall try every man's work, of what sort it is. If any man's work abide, which he had built thereupon, he shall receive a reward. If any man's work burn, he shall suffer loss; *but he himself shall be saved, yet so as by fire*" (*quasi per ignem*).

No man can lay any other foundation than on true faith in Jesus and all that he has taught—a lively, ardent faith; not a dead faith, but a faith working through charity, for "faith without good works is dead," St. James declares.

Having the sure foundation thus laid, every true Christian builds his own spiritual edifice thereon—his salvation and sanctification. These spiritual buildings vary in size, in strength, and in beauty, according to the greater or lesser spiritual knowledge, zeal, and holiness of the builders. Some build with "gold, silver, and precious stones"; these are the great Saints of God, who build with the pure gold of burning love, the shining silver of good, modest example, and the precious stones of heroic virtues. Others, not quite so elevated and holy in the sight of the Almighty, have but little silver, less gold, and scarcely any precious stones, but with no small quantity of wood, hay, and stubble. This is the class of ordinary good Christians, who strive to serve God, who perform many good actions during the course of their life, but who spoil them with wood, hay, stubble—that is to say, they perform them with negligence or with some vain and worldly motives mingled with the good, seeking after human applause or refraining from some holy deed for fear of worldly censure.

"The day of the Lord"—that is, the particular judgment after death—will make all this manifest, of what sort each man's work is; if he have built on a sure foundation and died in the friendship of God — although there might have been some "wood, hay, and stubble" by way of venial sins and imperfections—his soul will be saved, yet "so as by fire," and cleansed from all its dross and stains by the purifying fire of purgatory, and thus rendered fit for the presence of God. St.

Ambrose, commenting on this text, says: "Whereas St. Paul saith 'yet so as by fire,' he showeth, indeed, that he shall be saved, but yet shall suffer the punishment of fire; that, being purged by fire, he may be saved and not tormented for ever."

The gifted and deeply-learned Origen —a Greek Father of the second century— thus discourses on the same text: "For this cause, therefore, he that is saved is *saved by fire;* that if he happen to have anything of the nature of lead commingled with him, *that* the fire may burn and melt away, that all men may become pure gold, because the gold of the land, which the Saints are to preserve, is said to be pure; and 'as the furnace trieth gold, so doth temptation try the just' (Eccl. xxvii.) All, therefore, must come to the fire—all must come to the furnace. But, also, when we shall have come to that place, if any one shall have brought many good works and some little iniquity, that little is melted away and purified in the fire like lead, and all remains pure gold. And if any one have carried thither more lead, he suffers the fire more, that he may be the more refined, in order that, although there may be some little gold, the residue may still be pure. If any one should come thither all lead, that will be done to him which is written: 'He shall be swallowed down into the deep, like lead into the mighty waters' (Exodus xv.)

"There are sins which, when we commit them in ignorance, there is, I believe, decreed and prepared for us, by the command of God, a place where we must dwell for a certain time. . . . For be it that, after the *foundation, Christ Jesus*, in whom thou hast been instructed, thou hast built no abiding gold and silver and precious stones; thou mayest have gold, either much or little, even silver and precious stones, but also wood, hay, and stubble; what wouldst thou wish to become of thee after thy departure? Wouldst thou enter the holy places with thy wood, and thy hay, and thy stubble, thereby to defile the kingdom of God? Or, on the other hand, wouldst thou, on account of the wood, hay, and stubble, remain in the fire and receive nothing for the gold, silver, and precious stones? This is not just. The fire will consume the wood, the hay, the stubble; for God is a *consuming* fire."

In the First Epistle of St. Peter (iii.

18, 19) we learn that Christ "being put to death, indeed, in the flesh, but brought to life by the spirit, in which also He came and preached to those spirits who were in prison."

Our Blessed Saviour, immediately after death, descended into that part of hell called Limbo, and, as St. Peter informs us, "preached to the spirits who were in prison." This most certainly shows the existence of a middle state. The spirits to whom our Lord preached were certainly not in the hell of the damned, where His preaching could not possibly bear any fruit; they were not already in heaven, where no preaching is necessary, since there they see God face to face. Therefore they must have been in some middle state—call it by whatever name you please—where they were anxiously awaiting their deliverance at the hands of their Lord and Redeemer.

Belief in purgatory is more ancient than Christianity itself. It was the belief among the Jews of old, and of this we have clear proof in the Second Book of Machabees xii. 43. After a great victory gained by that valiant chieftain, Judas Machabeus, about two hundred years before the coming of Christ, " Judas making a gathering, he sent twelve thousand drachmas of silver to Jerusalem for sacrifice to be offered for the sins of the dead, thinking well and justly concerning the resurrection. . . . It is, therefore, a holy and wholesome thought to pray for the dead, that they may be loosed from their sins."

It is customary, even in our days, in Jewish synagogues, to erect tablets reminding those present of the lately deceased, in order that they may remember them in their prayers. Surely if there did not exist a place of purgation no prayers nor sacrifices would be of any avail to the departed. We find the custom of praying, of offering the Holy Sacrifice of the Mass for their spiritual benefit, more especially on their anniversaries, an universal practice among the primitive Christians of the Eastern and Western Churches, of the Greek, Latin, and Oriental rites.

Even if we did not find strong warrant, as we do, in the Scriptures, the authority of

APOSTOLIC TRADITION

would be amply sufficient for us; for, remember, we Catholics hold the traditions, handed down from the Apostles, to be of as much weight as their own writings.

Our Blessed Saviour did not build His Church on the Scriptures, but on the preaching of the Apostles. He wrote nothing Himself, nor did He command them to write. He did not say to the Apostles: Go and write the New Testament, and spread copies of it throughout the world; but "Go, teach all nations, instructing them to observe all things whatsoever I have commanded you; and, behold, I am with you all days, even unto the consummation of the world."

The different portions of the New Testament were written at different times, in different places, by different authors, and to suit the exigencies of different occasions. It was never intended to contain a complete system of the truths of revelation. It is undoubtedly the

WORD OF GOD,

and we revere it as such; but the Church had spread over a considerable part of the known world before the last Epistle of St. John the Evangelist was written—about the close of the first century, A.D. 99, according to Baronius. The different parts of the Bible were not joined together in one volume until the fifth century, when their canonicity was decided by a Council held in Rome under Pope Gelasius I., A.D. 494.

We revere the apostolic traditions preserved in the Church just as much as the apostolic writings. But some of our Protestant friends may say: "We do not want any of your traditions; we adhere to the Bible, and the Bible only, as it is the Word of God; and that is sufficient for us."

Well, we answer, How do you know that the Bible is the Word of God, that you have it pure and unadulterated as it left the hands of its inspired writers?

The oldest Protestant denomination only dates back three centuries—namely, to the sixteenth. The Bible was not written then, nor did it drop down from heaven. It must, then, have been from the Catholic Church that you received it —that Church in whose possession it was carefully preserved for the preceding fifteen centuries. It was copied year after year, and century after century, by pious and laborious monks, before the art of printing was discovered.

If bishops, priests, and monks were so

wicked as to invent the dogmas of "confession," the "intercession of Saints," and last, though not least, "purgatory," they could easily have corrupted the texts of the Bible.

There were no Protestants for fifteen centuries, and, under the circumstances supposed, there would have been none to protest against the corruption of the Word of God. Therefore there is at least one tradition (and that a Catholic one) you must hold—that the Bible is a divinely-inspired work—for you have no other possible way of discovering the fact. St. Augustine assures us that he would not believe in the Gospel, were it not for the authority of the Catholic Church.

Hence it is that we have recourse to sacred tradition as well as to Scripture for the proof of our teaching. With reference, then, to the doctrine of "purgatory," we are guided by the belief that prevailed among the primitive Christians.

That the custom of praying for the dead was sanctioned by the Apostles themselves we have the declaration of St. John Chrysostom: "It was not in vain instituted by the Apostles that in the celebration of the tremendous mysteries a remembrance should be made of the departed. They knew that much profit and advantage would be thereby derived."

Tertullian — the most ancient of the Latin Fathers, who flourished in the age immediately following that of the Apostles — speaks of the duty of a widow with regard to her deceased husband: "Wherefore also does she pray for his soul, and begs for him, in the interim, refreshment, and, in the first resurrection companionship, and makes offerings for him on the anniversary day of his falling asleep in the Lord. For unless she has done these things, she has truly repudiated him so far as is in her power." All this supposes a purgatory.

"The measure of the pain," says St. Gregory Nyssa, "is the quantity of evil to be found in each one. . . . Being either purified during the present life by means of prayer and the pursuit of wisdom, or, after departure from this life, by means of the furnace of the fire of purgation."

What more to the point, and at the same time what more touching, than the last charge of St. Monica to her noble and holy son, St. Augustine? "Lay this body anywhere; let not the care of it anyway disturb you; this only I request of you, that you will remember me at the Altar of the Lord, wherever you be."

In St. Augustine's beautiful prayer for his mother's repose we find a strong testimony to the doctrine of which we are treating:

"Although she, having been vivified in Christ, even when not as yet released from the flesh, so lived as that Thy Name is praised in her faith and manners, yet I dare not say that, from the time Thou didst regenerate her by baptism, no word has issued from her mouth against Thy precept. And it was said by the Truth, Thy Son: Whosoever shall say to his brother, Thou fool, shall be guilty of hell fire. And woe even to the praiseworthy life of men, if, laying aside mercy, Thou examine it. . . . I, therefore, O my praise and my life! having laid aside for a while her good actions, for which I give thanks to Thee with joy, do now beseech Thee for the sins of my mother; hear me through the Medicine of our wounds, Who hung upon the Wood, and Who, sitting at Thy right hand, maketh intercession for us. I know that she dealt mercifully, and from her heart forgave her debtors their debts; do Thou also forgive her her debts, if she contracted any during so many years after the waters of salvation. Forgive, O Lord! forgive, I beseech Thee."

In order to have a clear understanding of the doctrine of purgatory, a true idea of the teaching of the Church with regard to

SATISFACTION

is very necessary.

As was remarked before in one of the former papers, there is a close connection between all the truths of the Catholic system; and the principles laid down in one series of doctrines are carried to their legitimate, logical conclusion in the other. Speaking on the subject of confession, we said that there were three essential parts in the Sacrament of Penance—namely, contrition, confession, and satisfaction. Satisfaction in connection with that sacrament means or implies a fulfilment of whatever salutary penance the priest or confessor may impose, and it necessarily includes also something still more important—namely, that whatever injury may have been done to one's neighbor in person, property, or character must be fully repaired, or, at least, to the full extent of the penitent's ability. There is no forgiveness otherwise.

Stolen property must be restored to

its owner, injured character must be repaired, calumnies should be withdrawn even at the cost of the calumniator's own reputation, all just debts should be paid and all damage made good; otherwise the penitent need not expect forgiveness either here or hereafter.

Besides these satisfactions there is a general one incumbent on all who have sinned, even after having received pardon and remission.

Our Divine Lord offered up an infinite satisfaction for all, but, in order that it may be applied to our own individual souls, we must do our share, must show our appreciation of His infinite service by offering up our own penances and satisfactions. This has always been considered necessary by holy men in every age of the Christian era.

We believe that all the satisfactions of men and of angels for endless ages could never satisfy for one mortal sin or blot out the punishment due to it. This Jesus Christ alone can do; yet we believe at the same time that when, through His infinite merits, our sins are pardoned and their eternal guilt is washed away, there generally remains some

TEMPORAL PUNISHMENT

to be undergone in consequence. Adam and Eve sinned, and their sin was forgiven, yet what terrible calamities, by way of temporal punishment, fell on them and their descendants! This action of God goes to show, in a slight degree, how terrible all sin, especially grievous sin, is in His sight.

Moses and Aaron were dearly beloved

of God, and yet, in consequence of what we might consider a venial sin, a want of perfect confidence, they were obliged to undergo the punishment of not beholding the promised land: "And the Lord said to Moses and Aaron: Because you have not believed Me, to sanctify Me before the children of Israel, you shall not bring these people into the land which I will give them." And again: "Where the Lord spoke to Moses: Let Aaron, saith He, go to his people; for he shall not go into the land which I have given the children of Israel, because he was incredulous to my words at the waters of contradiction" (Numbers xx, Deut. xxxiv.)

So, in like manner, with regard to holy David, a man after God's own heart, who had the misfortune of committing two great sins; the Almighty sent His prophet Nathan to upbraid him for his crimes: "And David said to Nathan: I have sinned against the Lord. And Nathan said to David: The Lord hath also taken away thy sin; thou shalt not die." Here we find that David sinned and was forgiven, and his pardon was announced to him by a prophet of God. His sins were remitted; so, also, was the eternal punishment due to them; yet we know that he had to undergo a great temporal punishment for those very same offences the remission of which he obtained. "Nevertheless," says the prophet, "because thou hast given occasion to the enemies of the Lord to blaspheme for this thing, the child that is born to thee shall surely die" (2 Kings xii. 14).

When David committed a sin of vainglory in numbering his people, he repented of it; and, by way of temporal punishment, the Lord gave him his choice of three evils. David chose pestilence, and there died of his people seventy thousand men (2 Kings xxiv.)

The Scriptures inform us that David ate ashes like bread, mingled his tears with his drink, watered his couch by his weeping on account of his past sins, notwithstanding the divine assurance which he received that they were forgiven: "My sin is always before me"—*Peccatum meum contra me est semper.*

Thus sincere penitents in every age—before the coming of Christ and more especially since—have done rigorous penance for their past sins, bearing in mind the Scriptural injunction: "Be not without fear for sins forgiven."

They who have the highest appreciation of the sufferings and infinite merits of Jesus Christ are those who always make their utmost efforts to unite with His their own sufferings, satisfactions, works of penance and alms-deeds, in order that these may be rendered more acceptable in the sight of the Almighty, and thus avert those temporal afflictions He has in store for the sins we have committed, even though He has blotted out their eternal guilt. They who, in consequence of their holy lives, needed not such penance for themselves, offered it up, in union with the Sacrifice of their Saviour, for the benefit of their brethren; thus following the noble example of the Apostle Paul: "I now rejoice in my sufferings for you, and fill up those things that are wanting in the sufferings of Christ, for His body, which is the Church" (1

Colossians i. 24). Certainly there is nothing wanting in the sufferings of Christ Himself, as our Head; but His members are in need, and if they wish to enjoy the glory of their thorn-crowned Chief they must suffer with Him: "Through many tribulations we must enter the kingdom of heaven."

No one can be a true follower of Jesus Christ unless he follow Him on His way to Calvary: "If any man will come after Me, let him deny himself, take up his cross, and follow Me." It is one of the greatest and saddest of mistakes to imagine that, because our Saviour suffered for all men even unto the death of the Cross, we are thereby freed from the law of suffering or the obligation of doing penance. He calls us not to a life of ease and comfort, because He led a life of pain and ignominy for our sakes. He offered for us an infinite ransom, without which all the penance we might be able to do for ages could not avail, nor could it possibly bear any comparison with His infinite satisfaction; and yet we are not therefore dispensed from the duty of doing our own share, and offering it up to the Almighty in union with all that Jesus has done for us.

Even if this obligation existed not, we would be very ungrateful were we to lead a life of ease when He, the sinless One, led a life of hardship; to lead a life of pleasure, comfort, and luxury when He chose the rough way of the Cross, the hard and thorny road that led up to Calvary's mount, Calvary's torment, and Calvary's ignominy.

It has always been the belief of the

Church in every age that we all owe, in proportion to our sins, their number and grievousness, our own portion of satisfactory labor. This does not in the slightest degree detract from our Saviour's merits and infinite satisfaction, nor does it imbue the penitent with false notions in regard to his own self-sufficiency, as the Council of Trent expressly declares: "The satisfaction which we make for sin is not so ours, as if it were not through Jesus Christ; for we who can do nothing of ourselves, as of ourselves (2 Cor. iii. 5), can do all things in Him who strengthens us. Man, then, has nothing wherein to glory; but all our glory is in Christ, in whom we live, in whom we merit, in whom we make satisfaction, bringing forth fruits worthy of penance" (Session xiv. chap. viii.)

The farther we go back in ecclesiastical history and the nearer we approach the apostolic age, the more proof we find of the existence and practice of this belief among the earliest Christians. Besides confessing their sins publicly, they were obliged to undergo the most rigorous and prolonged penances. Sometimes for one grievous sin they had to perform public penance for three, five, ten, and twenty years, and even for a whole lifetime; to fast on bread and water, to remain outside the church doors, and to be deprived of the Sacraments unless in danger of death. The great Emperor Theodosius, for example, was stopped at the door of the Cathedral of Milan by its noble bishop, St. Ambrose, and was commanded to remain outside and do public penance for an act of great cruelty to a portion of his subjects.

So we see how deeply connected is the teaching of the Church on the necessity of satisfaction with the dogma of purgatory. They who fully satisfy here, who receive full and entire pardon of their sins, do penance in proportion to their offences, or suffer with Christian resignation, as coming from the hands of God, great trials and afflictions in this life, escape the punishment of purgatory in the next.

I have no difficulty in believing that there is a goodly number of faithful Christians here below who lead lives of poverty, ignominy, and contempt, who enjoy none of the good things of life, who are subject to misery from the cradle to the grave, who bear up under every hardship, trial, and affliction, serving God, at the same time, with "clean hands and pure hearts." I doubt not that they pass through their purgatory here, and will be immediately received after death into the loving embrace of their Lord and their God.

It would be unreasonable to suppose that others, believing Christians as they may be, but leading totally different lives, should have the same exemption or the same reward. They spend their days here in the enjoyment of the good things of this world; they have its comforts and its luxuries; they make little or no sacrifices; they fulfil their religious duties occasionally, or even frequently, but with little fervor; they sin, and sometimes grievously, and yet they deny themselves in nothing, but give themselves up to the vanities of life. They certainly do not pass through their purgatory here, and they may rest assured that, even if they have the good fortune of escaping hell, a long and painful purgatory awaits them in the next life before they shall be permitted to enter the abode of the blessed. All this stands to reason, and it becomes all the more clear when we consider another class to be found in every community.

Our Divine Lord declared that "it is easier for a camel to enter the eye of a needle than for a rich man to enter the kingdom of heaven." What is impossible to men is possible with the grace of God. All of which shows that it is only with great difficulty that such men may be saved. Riches are very frequently an occasion of sin to their possessors, since by them they may easily procure for themselves pleasures that are unlawful; and, moreover, since they render them often hard-hearted towards the poor. "Woe to you, ye rich!" says our Lord, "for you have your consolation here."

Let us consider some persons of this class, or of the class who make their whole life consist in the mere pursuit of sensual pleasures. They may have the true faith, and a certain amount of reverence for God and the things of God. They lead careless, and even sinful, lives. They indulge in many excesses. They constantly postpone their conversion from day to day, from youth to manhood, from manhood to old age, and even in old age itself until their death-bed. A real conversion then is indeed very rare. Many delude themselves with an imaginary conversion, and only find out their mistake when it is too late; that is, when they appear before the tribunal of God and are for ever condemned.

However, let us take it for granted that God, in His infinite mercy, bestows the grace of true conversion on one of the class of which we have been treating; that he dies in the grace of that Supreme Being to whom he had been an enemy the greater part of his life. Dying in His friendship, he of course escapes eternal damnation; but could any reasonable man say that such a one were fit, sufficiently pure to enjoy immediately the vision of God face to face—that All-holy Being before whom all that is impure must fly away, and into whose presence nothing defiled can enter?

Oh! no. God is a God of justice as

well as of mercy. Long, weary years shall pass, and even centuries, before some souls will be sufficiently purified by the fiery bath of purgatory, before they will be cleansed from all dross and alloy of sin and passion.

All our satisfactions here are voluntary, and consequently meritorious; a little here suffices for much hereafter, for *there* no one can possibly merit. "Amen, I say to thee, thou shalt not go out from thence until thou pay the last farthing." The doctrines of satisfaction and purgatory are productive of the most beneficial results. They teach us how to shape our lives accordingly. We learn to know the value of prayer, almsdeeds, penance, and more especially of suffering. Affliction is the great crucible for the refining, purifying, and spiritualizing of our immortal souls. No matter how or whence they proceed, we acknowledge all our trials and sorrows as coming from the hands of Him who "doth all things well"; and if we but bear them in the proper spirit, as satisfaction for our sins and in union with Christ's sufferings, we may rest assured that we are shortening the time of our purgatorial banishment. We become satisfied with whatever position in which we are placed by God; we bear with toil and hardship, the inconveniences as well as the miseries of life; and even in what appears our very misfortunes we kiss the hand that strikes us and bow down to the will of Him who afflicts us. We know full well that "God chastises those whom He loves," and that it is far better to be chastised here than hereafter; for here His *mercy* reigns, hereafter His *justice*.

Most miserable and truly to be pitied is the man who seems happy and prosperous in this life, and who, at the same time, lives a stranger to God and His grace, adding sin to sin, and treasuring up "wrath against the day of wrath." All his punishment is before him, and eternal misery awaits him. On a sudden the wrath of God shall come upon him, and darkness shall be his portion for ever

Truly blessed is he who, after he has done grievous wrong in the sight of the Almighty, is visited immediately with chastisement, and is thus recalled to a sense of his duty, bemoans his sinfulness, and turns once more to God with greater earnestness than before. Then may it be said of such, as of Mary Magdalen:

"Much hath been forgiven her, because she hath loved much."

If we desire to escape purgatory we should spend holy lives here, mortify our passions, subdue our appetites, deny ourselves in many things, even though permitted, in order that we might the more easily control our inclinations in what is unlawful, thus making at the same time some satisfaction for our past offences.

Not only deeply instructive but also

EMINENTLY CONSOLING

is the doctrine of purgatory. We need not "mourn as those who have no hope," for those nearest and dearest who have gone hence and departed this life in the friendship of God.

How beautifully our Holy Mother the Church bridges over the terrible chasm of the grave! How faithfully and tenderly she comes to our aid in the saddest of our griefs and sorrows! She leaves us not to mourn uncomforted, unsustained. She chides us not for shedding tears over our dear lost ones—a beloved parent, a darling child, a loving brother, affectionate sister, or deeply-cherished friend or spouse. She bids us let our tears flow, for our Saviour wept at the grave of Lazarus.

She whispers words of comfort—not unmeaning words, but words of divine hope and strength—to our breaking hearts. She pours the oil of heavenly consolation into our deepest wounds. She bids us cast off all unseemly grief, assuring us that not even death itself can sever the bond that unites us; that we can be of service to those dear departed ones whom we loved better than life itself; that we can aid them by our prayers and good works, and especially by the Holy Sacrifice of the Mass. Thus may we abridge their days of banishment, assuage their pains, and continue to storm heaven itself with our piteous appeals until the Lord deign to look down in mercy, open their prison-doors, and admit them to the full light of His holy presence and to the everlasting embrace of their Redeemer and their God.

VI.

INFALLIBILITY.

AN was created in original justice, and with the full and perfect use of all his faculties. Having fallen from his high estate, his intellect became weakened and his will disordered. The faculties of reason had no longer their legitimate control over the faculties of sense. Man, depending solely on himself, fell to his lowest state.

For four thousand years the world, with the exception of the Jewish people—the depositaries of God's revelation and promises — tried the experiment of living without God or a true knowledge of the relations existing between the Creator and the creature. Slowly but surely did the nations of the earth lose their earliest traditions of religion and sink into the most fearful corruption of soul and body. It became evident that man could not be saved by science or art, statesmanship or even philosophy. The fulness of time, no doubt, had come for God to assume our nature and manifest Himself to His creatures. Jesus Christ, the Divine Word Incarnate, came on earth for no other purpose than to offer up an infinite ransom for our souls, and to point out the true path that leads to everlasting happiness. In His infinite goodness and mercy He condescended to our low estate, to become man like unto us, in order that He might secure us the means by which we could surely follow in His footsteps and become partakers of His unspeakable reward.

For this purpose He established a Church, which He made the depository not only of the infinite merits acquired by His sufferings and death, but the depository likewise of all those truths which He came to announce unto mankind—not simply to one race or people, or age or country, but to all tribes and nations and all succeeding ages unto the end of time.

Had He not come to show us the way, then we would be free to choose our own; but having come, out of infinite condescension, it is evidently His intention that we should all select the path which He so clearly marked out for us. "Wishing all men to be saved and to arrive at the knowledge of truth," as the Apostle declares, He no doubt places means within their reach for attaining this knowledge and saving truth.

We all believe that Jesus Christ, being the Incarnate God, must be infinitely wise, as He is also infinitely powerful. Desiring to attain the end which He proposed unto Himself, He must necessarily have adapted the means unto the end. Hence He must have established a rule of faith that would suit all ages, all characters, all dispositions, that would be applicable to every people and suit the exigencies of all time.

THE RULE OF FAITH

should be a plain one, easily discerned, easily grasped, adapted to the weakest as well as the strongest minds, as binding on the learned and powerful as on the uneducated and lowly. It should be not only a plain rule but also a comprehensive one, embracing all necessary truths, all important doctrines; and a perfectly safe and sure rule, so that no one might be led into error on points of faith or practice.

Isaias prophesied that when the Redeemer should come He would point out the way—the way of holiness, a certain and sure way, which no one could mistake, and even fools could not fail to perceive, and leading to eternal happiness: "And a path and a way shall be there, and it shall be called the holy way; the unclean shall not pass over it, and this shall be unto you a straight way, so that fools shall not err therein. . . . And the redeemed of the Lord shall return, and shall come into Sion with praise, and everlasting joy shall be upon their heads; they shall obtain joy and gladness, and sorrow and mourning shall flee away" (xxxv. 8, 10).

They who believe in the divinity of Christ and His mission cannot but admit that He was wise enough to institute a religion, establish a Church or system of divine truth, which would suit the requirements of every age, be a rule to all classes of men without distinction, and a sure and infallible guide for all generations unto the end of the world. That He was wise enough to devise such a Church, and powerful enough to carry out His design, no Christian can call into doubt.

The sure rule of faith was to be

A LIVING, INFALLIBLE TEACHER.

For our Saviour, as we said in the preceding treatise, did not found His Church on the Sacred Scriptures, but on the preaching of His Word by the Apostles. The Bible is the infallible Word of God; it is the rule of faith, but not the *only* rule. It does not contain all revealed truth, nor was it intended ever so to do. Christians, as a body, believe many things for which they can find no proof in the Bible; for instance, you cannot prove by the Bible why you observe Sunday and keep it holy, instead of the Sabbath, or seventh day, commanded in the Sacred Scriptures.

2. The Apostles strictly forbade the eating of blood or things strangled (Acts xv. 29), and you cannot prove from their writings that you are dispensed from the obligation.

3. You cannot prove from the Bible

itself the canonicity or the divine inspiration of its component parts.

Our Blessed Saviour no doubt said: "Search the Scriptures," or, according to the more correct version: "You search the Scriptures." But these words were addressed to the Scribes and Pharisees, who denied His divine mission, and whom He consequently referred to the Old Testament, to the writings of Moses and the prophets, "who gave testimony of Him." He certainly did not refer to the New Testament, not one word of which was written until several years after His death. He Himself wrote nothing, nor do we anywhere find that He commanded anything to be written. The majority of the Apostles left no writings after them; and those of them who did write, it was only after they had founded their churches, to satisfy particular requests or to meet certain emergencies. All the early Christian churches were founded by the preaching of the Gospel, and not by the diffusion of copies of the Scriptures. As St. Irenæus, who lived in the age immediately following that of the Apostles, declared: Gentes barbaræ sine litteris fidem didicerunt—"Foreign nations learned the faith without the aid of letters."

The vast majority of people, in all ages of the Christian era, were unable to read; and, even if they had been able, it would have been impossible, except for the most wealthy, to procure a copy of a large work like the Bible—in manuscript, of course, as the art of printing was not discovered until the middle of the fifteenth century. It is only four hundred and twenty-four years since the Bible was first printed by the Catholic Gutenberg.

So we see most clearly that the Bible was not, and could not possibly have been, the only rule of faith for

SO MANY GENERATIONS

who were obliged to receive their faith from the oral instructions of their pastors, who explained to them the Word of God and the different mysteries of the Catholic Religion. If the Almighty intended that the Sacred Scriptures should be the only rule of faith, He would not have permitted the discovery of the art of printing, so necessary for His supposed design, to have been kept in the dark so many hundreds of years.

And now that, by reason of the printing-press, copies of the Bible are spread with greatest profusion over the face of the earth, it does not prove itself to be the sure, certain, and unmistakable rule, since even the learned differ so much as to its interpretation.

How can those who believe not in the Catholic Church be sure that they have the Bible pure and unadulterated, neither added to nor diminished from what it was when it left the hands of its inspired writers; that the translation they possess is a faithful rendering of the original? An examination of this kind would take the most of a man's lifetime; would require immense labor, very deep study, and no small amount of ability, as well as a correct knowledge of various different languages. Surely such could not have been the means adopted by an All-wise Redeemer for the salvation of the human race.

No *sure faith* can be derived from the Bible without a *sure teacher*. Of what practical use could be the infallible Word, the dead letter of the law, without the living voice of an infallible interpreter? What advantage was to be derived from the coming of Christ upon earth to establish but one true Church, if every Christian were free to form his own creed, to draw his own faith from the Bible, to be guided by no authority but his own judgment, to receive and accept what he liked, to reject what he disliked—whatever did not agree with his fancies, his whims, his pet theories, or even his passions and prejudices?

Erect private judgment as the standard, the rule of faith, and there is no authority on earth to which a man is obliged to submit. All other churches except the Catholic confess that they are fallible, or liable to err; and, in making this admission, they cannot reasonably demand for their various creeds or professions of faith the perfect assent of mind of their followers.

Admit the right of private judgment in the interpretation of the Scriptures, and you concede at the same time the right to every man to establish a church of his own, if he be not pleased with any of those already founded. For most certainly, if one man have the right of seceding from the Church and forming a creed of his own, a sect or denomination, every other individual has the same right. Hence it is now almost impossible to count the number of so-called religions. We hear of some new one being *invented* nearly every month. It was only a few years ago since the body styling itself the Reformed Episcopal Church separated from the Protestant Episcopal Churches of England and America; and it was only very lately we learned from the public journals that Dr. Gregg, who became bishop of that church, separated from that also and formed a new one of his own, of which he constituted himself the Primate. In fact, he intends to be Pope of it—and small blame to him; for if he have the power of establishing a new religion, no one can very well dispute his title to be its supreme pontiff.

So it will be unto the end of time. New sects will constantly arise to lead men far away from the truth so long as poor, weak, erring mortals will attempt to improve on the work of God in the establishment of a church.

Our Lord and Saviour Jesus Christ established but

ONE TRUE CHURCH,

"the pillar and ground of truth," and He founded it on a Rock that was never to fail, never to be submerged amid the waves of error, heresy, or corruption—the imperishable Rock of Ages, which no storm can shake or move from its unshifting, unchangeable foundations, and against which, He most solemnly declared, all the powers of hell shall never prevail: "And I say to thee: Thou art Peter [a rock], and on this rock I will build my Church, and the gates of hell shall not prevail against it" (St. Matthew xvi. 18).

What is meant by the "gates of hell"

but the powers of darkness, all errors, heresies, schisms, all efforts of human as well as diabolic malice?

That Jesus Christ made this solemn promise no one can doubt, since it is found in all versions of the Bible. He likewise promised to send, for the guidance of the Apostles and their successors, His Holy Spirit, who would teach them all truth and recall to their minds whatsoever He had taught them; and that He Himself would remain with them all days, "even unto the consummation of the world."

Was Jesus Christ able to fulfil His promises, or was He not? If not, then He was not the divine person He claimed to be; and *quod nimis probat, nihil probat*—what proves too much proves nothing for our adversaries, as in that case all Christianity falls to the ground as the hugest of impositions.

If Christ were able to fulfil his promises, then the Catholic Church stands on the same foundation it ever did, and so shall it remain unto the end of time, the infallible Teacher of mankind, to whose instructions all men, whether learned or unlearned, should immediately submit.

If error or heresy ever crept into its authoritative teaching, if ever for any period of time, be it a century or be it simply one moment, it fell away from the true faith of Christ, then most undoubtedly "the gates of hell" prevailed against it and the promises of Christ most miserably failed. If His promises failed, then He was not a divine person; if not a divine person, then not even a good man, but the most successful of deceivers and most arrant of impostors. There is no logical standing ground between the two parts of this proposition.

We believe, then, that the Catholic Church was gifted with

INFALLIBILITY

by its Divine Founder—that is to say, it never erred and never can err in matters of faith or morals; it can never propose or define any doctrine as a dogma that has not been handed down from Christ and His Apostles, and contained explicitly, or at least implicitly, in the original deposit of faith.

We believe, moreover, that with whatever infallibility the Church is endowed, so is its visible head, the Bishop of Rome,

THE SUCCESSOR OF ST. PETER.

In other words, the Pope, the Vicegerent of Christ, when speaking *ex cathedra*, as Head of the Church, in defining dogma or morals, cannot err in his teaching.

A great many persons mistake *infallibility* for *impeccability*. There is a vast difference between them. Impeccable means that a person cannot sin. Now, no Catholic, be he never so little instructed in the faith, believes that the Pope cannot sin. The Pope is a weak man like ourselves, subject to the same passions, the same evil inclinations, the same temptations as we. He has to make use of the same safeguards, and, in fact, greater safeguards than the majority of Christians, for he is placed higher, "in alto positus," and has more fearful responsibilities. Popes may sin, and some have sinned. Nor is this wonderful; for since there was one faithless Apostle among the twelve, we need not be surprised that there were a few—very few indeed—among the Sovereign Pontiffs who were unworthy of their exalted position.

So a Pope is liable to sin, and, as a private teacher, in ordinary conversation or in familiar discourse he is also liable to say what may be erroneous.

He is infallible or preserved from error, through the promise of Christ and the gracious assistance of the Holy Spirit, only when he addresses the whole Church, as its Head, on what appertains to faith or morals.

The Pope cannot invent any new doctrine, cannot promulgate as a dogma what has no foundation in Sacred Writ or in apostolic tradition. He decides or defines what has been always believed in the Church from the very beginning, whenever it seems necessary or exceedingly beneficial to make a dogma of a truth already believed, but subject to discussions or controversies injurious to the piety or obedience of the faithful. Three examples of this may here be given: The divinity of Christ, for instance, was undoubtedly believed by all true Christians from the very foundation of the Church, and yet it was not declared a dogma until the Council of Nice, A.D. 325, and then only because of the injurious and seductive teaching of the Arians. So also the Immaculate Conception of the Blessed Virgin Mary and the Infallibility of the Pope are doctrines that have always been believed in the Church, with but few dissenting voices, and still they were not declared dogmas, under pain of excommunication, until our own time.

The vast majority of Catholics believe now, and always did believe, that the Blessed Virgin immediately after death was taken up, body and soul, into heaven, and yet it is not a dogma of faith. Suppose that in a hundred years from now it should be proclaimed a dogma, it could not be then said that it is a new doctrine.

Let us now examine the grounds on which the dogma of

PAPAL INFALLIBILITY.

rests, and give a reason for the faith that is in us.

Destining His Church to last during all time, our Divine Lord built it on such a foundation as would resist all the storms of ages and all the machinations of its enemies. He commissioned twelve Apostles to preach His Gospel unto every people: "Go, teach all nations"; and He endowed them with all the powers and faculties necessary for the successful fulfilment of His most holy design. The like powers that were given to Him by His Heavenly Father He bestowed on them and their successors: "As the Father hath sent Me, I also send you." Giving unto them this wonderful and divine power, He knew full well, for He knew all things, that the Church was not to end with His Apostles, but, through their successors, to continue unto the consummation of ages. He consequently determined on establishing

A CENTRE OF UNITY

for the whole Christian world, and thus

prevent any schisms, heresies, or spirit of disunion from ever sundering that bond of union which was to be during all time the distinguishing mark or characteristic of the One True Church.

Granting full and ample powers to all the Apostles in order to carry out their mission of converting the nations, He conferred the Primacy, with all its honor, authority, and prerogatives, on St. Peter alone, whom He constituted the Head or Chief of the Apostolic band. This is fully proved from Christ's own words as contained in the Gospel, the testimony of all Christian antiquity, and the practice as well as belief of the universal Church.

Three different times, and in the most solemn manner, did Christ bestow this special authority and exalted privilege on

St. Peter: 1. When St. Peter, first of all the Apostles, confessed his faith openly in the divinity of his Master: "Jesus saith to them: But whom do ye say that I am? Simon Peter answering, said to Him: Thou art Christ, the Son of the living God. And Jesus answering, said to him: Blessed art thou, Simon Bar-Jona; because flesh and blood hath not revealed it to thee, but My Father who is in heaven. And I say to thee: that thou art Peter, and upon this rock I will build My Church; and the gates of hell shall not prevail against it. And I will give to thee the keys of the kingdom of heaven; and whatsoever thou shalt bind upon earth, it shall be bound also in heaven; and whatsoever thou shalt loose upon earth, it shall be loosed also in heaven" (Matt. xvi. 15-19).

To St. Peter alone were given

"THE KEYS OF THE KINGDOM,"

which words, according to the manner of speaking among the people of the East, most forcibly denoted the conferring of supreme power and authority. This is the sense in which it is used by Isaias, xxii. 22: "And I will lay the *key of the house of David* upon his shoulder: and he shall open, and none shall shut: and he shall shut, and none shall open." Also by St. John in the Apocalypse, or Revelations, iii. 7: "These things saith the Holy One and True One, who hath the *key of David:* He that openeth, and no man shutteth; and shutteth, and no man openeth."

On account of his noble confession of faith the Lord changed Simon's name to Peter—Kipho in Syriac, Cephas in

Greek, and Petrus from the Latin *petra*, which signifies a rock; thus meriting to become *the rock* on which the Church was to be built—the immovable rock of the Papacy, impregnable against all the storms of error and heresy. "And the rain fell, and the floods came, and the winds blew, and they beat upon that house, and it fell not, for it was founded upon a rock" (St. Matt. vii. 25).

Origen, who lived in the third century, says that "Peter was by the Lord called a rock, since to him is said: 'Thou art Peter, and on this rock I will build My Church.' The chief authority as regards the feeding of the flock was delivered to Peter."

"Who can be ignorant," says St. Augustine, "that the most blessed Peter is the Chief of the Apostles?"

The second time to which reference is made is as follows: We know full well that Christ's prayer is always heard, as He Himself declared: "Father, I give Thee thanks that Thou hast heard Me, and I know that Thou hearest Me always" (St. John xi. 41). There is no doubt that He prayed most particularly for Peter and all his successors in office, that his faith and theirs might be always constant and true, so that they should be the leaders and confirmers of their brethren during all time: "Simon, Simon, behold Satan hath desired to have thee that he may sift thee as wheat: but I have prayed for thee that thy faith fail not; and thou being once converted, confirm thy brethren" (St. Luke xxii. 31, 32).

The faith of the See of Peter has

never failed and never shall fail; for on the Rock of Peter, as on a sure, solid, enduring foundation, Christ built His Church.

3. After our Lord's glorious Resurrection, and immediately before His Ascension, by the Sea of Galilee He gave full charge to St. Peter of the whole Church —the entire flock, both shepherds and sheep—to feed them with the heavenly food of true doctrine, to dispense the mysteries of God, to watch over, govern, direct, and guide the one true fold for whose salvation He, the Good Shepherd, laid down His life.

There and then he required a triple affirmation from St. Peter of his love towards Him, and with a triple charge did the Saviour command him to feed His whole flock: " Jesus saith to Simon

Peter: Simon, Son of John, lovest thou Me more than these? He saith to Him: Yea, Lord, Thou knowest that I love Thee. He saith to him: Feed My lambs. He saith to him again: Simon, son of John, lovest thou Me? He saith to Him: Yea, Lord, Thou knowest that I love Thee. He saith to him: Feed My lambs. He saith to him the third time: Simon, son of John, lovest thou Me? Peter was grieved, because He said to him the third time, Lovest thou Me? And he said to Him: Lord, Thou knowest all things: Thou knowest that I love Thee. He said to him: Feed My sheep" (St. John xxi. 15-17).

This comparison of His Church to a flock was a favorite one of our Lord, as we may see from the tenth chapter of the Gospel according to St. John:

"And other sheep I have, that are not of this fold: them also I must bring; they shall hear My voice, and there shall be one fold and one shepherd." Such was to be for ever the distinctive mark of His Church, by which it may be infallibly known from all others: "There shall be *one fold* and *one shepherd.*"

The words of our Saviour constituting St. Peter the visible head of the Church and the shepherd of the *one fold* were well understood by the Apostles themselves. In their sacred writings they invariably give the first place to St. Peter whenever they mention him in connection with the others; he is always the spokesman—the organ, so to speak—of the Apostolic College: "Now the names of the twelve Apostles are these: the first, Simon, who is called Peter" (St. Matt.

x. 2.) But some one might say that the Evangelist enumerated them in the order in which they were called to the faith. In that case St. Peter should not be named first, but his brother, St. Andrew; therefore this objection falls to the ground. There are a number of other texts in this connection: "And *Simon* and they who were with him" (St. Mark i. 36); "*Peter* and they who were with him" (St. Luke ix. 32).

St. Peter was the first to preach to the people after the descent of the Holy Ghost on the apostolic band the day of Pentecost: "*Peter* standing up with the eleven, lifted up his voice and spoke to them" (Acts of Apostles ii. 14).

Again, chapter v. 29: "*Peter* then answering and the apostles, said." So also at the first council of the Church, held at Jerusalem, when "the Apostles and ancients came together to consider of this matter. And when there was much disputing, *Peter* rising up, said, etc. . . . And all the multitude held their peace" (xv. 7, 12).

Our Saviour taught the multitude from the bark of Peter (Luke v. 3), and continues so to do during all succeeding ages. We learn from St. Matthew (xvii. 26) that our Lord paid tribute for Himself and Peter.

Most assuredly all this did not happen without design, and that design the evident intention of Christ to constitute Peter, and his successors in the Apostolic See, the centre of unity and the source of all power, authority, and jurisdiction for the entire Church.

St. Peter was the first of the Apostles

to whom the Lord appeared after His Resurrection; the first to open the council, to work the first miracle, and the first to call both Jews and Gentiles to the faith.

The primacy of honor and jurisdiction, and the prerogatives attached thereto, were always acknowledged in the Church from the very beginning as being the inherent rights of the occupant of the See of Peter.

That St. Peter established his See at Rome, and from there exercised rule over the whole Church, is as well established a fact as any other important event in history. St. Irenæus, who flourished in the second century, enumerating the bishops of Rome, says: "St. Peter succeeded Linus; to Linus, Anacletus; then, in the third place, Clement." Besides other historical proofs we have the testimonies of Eusebius, the Father of ecclesiastical history; of the learned St. Jerome, and the most ancient Calendarium Romanum.

Eusebius thus speaks: "The providence of the Universal Ruler led, as it were by the hand, to Rome Peter, the great one and most powerful of the Apostles, and, on account of his virtue, the mouthpiece of the others against that sad destroyer of the human race (Simon Magus). He (Peter), like a noble general appointed by God, armed with heavenly weapons, brought the precious merchandise of intellectual light from the East to the dwellers in the West." This fact is admitted by the most learned of our opponents—Pearson, Usher, Cave, and others.

St. Jerome, writing to Pope Damasus,

thus expresses himself on this point: "I am following no other than Christ, united to the communion of Your Holiness—that is, to the Chair of Peter. I know that the Church is founded on that rock. Whoever eateth the Lamb out of that House is a profane man. Whoever is not in the ark shall perish by the flood. . . . He that gathereth not with you, scattereth."

St. Augustine declared that what kept him in the Catholic Church was "the succession of priests from the very Chair of Peter—to whom the Lord, after His Resurrection, committed His flock to be fed—down to the present bishop."

"In the city of Rome," says St. Optatus (fourth century), "on Peter was the episcopal chair first conferred, that, in one chair, unity might be preserved by all."

Whoever, then, would dare deny this fact would obtain as little credit as he who should deny that Washington was the first President of the United States. One is as much an absolute fact of history as the other.

All acknowledge that the Jewish Synagogue was but a figure of the Church of Christ, and that the figure can bear no comparison in perfection with the reality. In the Old Law, then, a special direction and assistance were vouchsafed to the High-Priest (Deut. xvii. 9). How much more is this special guidance due to the chief representative and Vicar of Jesus Christ in the New Law—the law of grace and perfection!

1. It is a matter of history that never since the foundation of the Church has any Pope (no matter what his private

character may have been) broached any heresy when speaking *ex cathedra*, as Head of the Church universal.

2. Papal decisions on matters of faith, morals, or even discipline have been received in all ages with the greatest respect, reverence, and obedience by the great body of pastors of the Church. In the early ages Pope Clement corrected abuses in the Church of Corinth, Pope Victor in that of Ephesus, and Pope Stephen in that of Africa.

3. Heresies in different ages were condemned by Popes acting on their own authority and without the aid of councils.

4. No council has ever been considered *œcumenical* unless it was presided over by the Pope or his delegates, or had his approbation as to its decrees. The Fathers of the Council of Chalce-

don, on hearing the letter of Pope Leo read to them, exclaimed: "This is the faith of our fathers: Peter has spoken through Leo."

5. In difficulties of any magnitude appeals from bishops, and even patriarchs, were always laid before the Pope. Pope Julius restored Paul, Patriarch of Constantinople, and Athanasius, Patriarch of Alexandria, to their respective sees; and Pope Innocent reinstated the great St. John Chrysostom.

Never was there a time when

THE PAPACY

attracted so much attention and was the object of so much investigation as at present. All eyes are turned towards it. Every part of its history, every minute particular, is examined. Learning, science, history, and research have made their utmost endeavors to solve the mystery of its existence. Love and hatred, confidence and mistrust, have been exercised in its favor or disfavor, and yet it stands the wonder of all, the miracle of the universe.

Without the Papacy there would be no Catholicity, as there would be no Catholicity without unity. The centre of unity is the Chair of Peter, the Apostolic See, the fountain of ecclesiastical authority, the source of spiritual jurisdiction. It is a

DIVINE ORGANISM,

living its own life, and imparting light and heat to the whole world. It is the creation of God. It derives not its power from men; it owes not its existence to any agreement or compact. It is the heart as well as head of the Church. Life and light radiate from that divinely-appointed centre. Any member not united with that Head, not animated by that Heart, is dead—cannot live its true life or attain its true destiny. *Ubi Petrus, ibi Ecclesia*—where Peter is, there is the Church—says St. Ambrose. No one can be a member of the Catholic Church who is not in communion with the See of Peter. This is an indispensable requisite.

Whoever is not in accord with the faith of Peter—for Peter lives in each of his successors—cannot be a member of Christ, who is the invisible Head of the Church, as the Pope, the Bishop of Rome, is its visible Head and His Vice-gerent: "He who will not hear the Church," says our Lord, "let him be to thee as a heathen and a publican." "For the lips of the priest," says the prophet Malachy, "shall keep knowledge, and they shall seek the law at his mouth; because he is the angel of the Lord of Hosts" (Mal. ii. 7). "He that knoweth God, heareth us: he that is not of God, heareth us not; by this we know the spirit of truth, and the spirit of error," says St. John (1 Epistle iv. 6).

"There are other sheep," our Blessed Saviour says, "not of the fold," whom He is anxious to lead in, that they may be made *one fold* under the *one* shepherd.

There are many, I believe, outside the fold not through any fault of their own. They have been brought up in ignorance of, and oftentimes embittered against, that faith into which, although unconsciously on their part, they have been baptized. For, let it be well understood, when a person is validly baptized, no matter by whom, he becomes *ipso facto* a member of the Holy Catholic Church, and such he remains until, by some act of his own free will, he rejects the known truth and adheres to some heresy.

Hence I trust that there are many joined with us in *spiritual*, who are, to all appearances, far from us in *bodily*, communion. And yet it is their duty to enquire, to investigate, to examine on what grounds they rest their faith; and, above all, to pray frequently to the Almighty, to implore most earnestly the light of the Holy Spirit, that He may discover to them the whole truth as it is in Christ Jesus, and that he may give them the grace to follow whithersoever He may lead. Let them live lives of purity and prayer, and exercise generous charity towards the poorer members of Jesus Christ, and they may rest assured that He will forsake them not in the time of need nor leave their prayers unanswered.

In conclusion, let me beg of all who differ from us to cast aside all prejudice and bigotry, and to examine calmly, like earnest men and Christians, the claims of the Catholic Church on their studious attention. I assure them, with all the sincerity of my soul, that there is no study in the world of deeper interest or more worthy of their consideration.

No other investigation can bring forth so rich a fruit, so happy a result. The deeper we advance into that Holy of Holies the more the clouds that seemed to shadow its entrance vanish from sight and disappear, until the full splendor of God's truth and God's light shine upon our souls, dispelling all doubt, and every shadow of doubt, and holding our minds entranced beyond power of resistance.

Such is the Catholic Church to those who know it as it is, and who love it as the

ever faithful spouse

of Jesus Christ, without "spot or wrinkle," stain or imperfection—"Thou art all fair, my dove, and there is no stain in thee," as the Divine One says to His beloved in the Canticle of Canticles.

The more I study the Catholic Faith the more and more am I ravished with its beauty all divine, its heavenly dogmas, its sublime moral code, its eminent reasonableness, and perfect adaptability to all the needs of man's nature, all the aspirations of his immortal soul.

Therefore it is that, being so deeply convinced of its divine mission unto the whole human race, I long with the soul's inmost longing for others to enjoy the same inestimable privileges, to be blessed with the same divine faith, to be brought by God's all-powerful grace into that one true fold at the gate of which Jesus Christ, the Good Shepherd, stands, anxiously waiting to embrace them in His outstretched Fatherly arms.

"The grace of Our Lord Jesus Christ, and the charity of God, and the communication of the Holy Spirit be with you all." Amen.